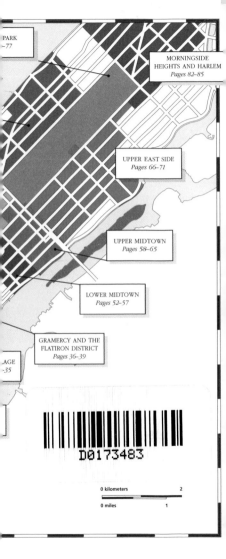

PARK
–77

MORNINGSIDE
HEIGHTS AND HARLEM
Pages 82–85

UPPER EAST SIDE
Pages 66–71

UPPER MIDTOWN
Pages 58–65

LOWER MIDTOWN
Pages 52-57

GRAMERCY AND THE
FLATIRON DISTRICT
Pages 36–39

AGE
–35

0 kilometers   2

0 miles   1

EYEWITNESS TRAVEL

NEW YORK

POCKET GUIDE

DK

LONDON, NEW YORK,
MELBOURNE, MUNICH AND DELHI
www.dk.com

PROJECT DIRECTORS Nicholas Bevan, Derek Hall

EDITORS Derek Hall, Marion Dent, Sue Juby

DESIGNERS Richard Evans

INDEXER Michael Dent

PICTURE RESEARCHER Mirco De Cet

CARTOGRAPHY John Plumer, Dave Brooker, Paul Hopgood

Conceived and produced by Redback Publishing, 25 Longhope
Drive, Farnham, Surrey, GU10 4SN

Reproduced by Colourscan (Singapore)

Printed and bound in China by Leo Paper Products Ltd.

First published in Great Britain in 2006
by Dorling Kindersley Limited
80 Strand, London WC2R 0RL

A CIP CATALOGUE RECORD IS AVAILABLE FROM THE BRITISH LIBRARY.

ISBN-13: 978-1-40531–355-1

ISBN-10: 1-40531-35 5-2

The information in this
DK Eyewitness Travel Guide is checked regularly.

Every effort has been made to ensure that this book is as up-to-date as
possible at the time of going to press. Some details, however, such as
telephone numbers, opening hours, prices, gallery hanging
arrangements and travel information, are liable to change. The
publishers cannot accept responsibility for any consequences arising
from the use of this book, nor for any material on third-party websites,
and cannot guarantee that any website address in this book will be a
suitable source of travel information. We value the views and
suggestions of our readers highly. Please write to:
Publisher, DK Eyewitness Travel Guides,
Dorling Kindersley, 80 Strand, London WC2R 0RL.

Brooklyn bridge with the Manhattan skyscrapers behind

CONTENTS

INTRODUCING NEW YORK

Manhattan **4**

New York's Highlights **6**

NEW YORK AREA BY AREA

Lower Manhattan **8**

Seaport and the
Civic Center **16**

Lower East Side **20**

Soho and Tribeca **24**

Greenwich Village **28**

East Village **32**

Gramercy and the
Flatiron District **36**

Chelsea and the
Garment District **40**

Theater District **46**

Lower Midtown **52**

Upper Midtown **58**

Upper East Side **66**

Central Park **72**

Upper West Side **78**

Morningside Heights
and Harlem **82**

Farther Afield **86**

PRACTICAL INFORMATION

Getting Around **90**

Survival Guide **92**

Index **94**

Acknowledgments **96**

Steel public sculpture by Louise Nevelson, Park Avenue

Manhattan

Most of the sights in this book lie within 15 areas of Manhattan, part of the non-stop, 24-hour city of New York. Thrill to its great skyscrapers, shop on glittering Fifth Avenue, soak up culture along Museum Mile, relax in Central Park, eat soul food in Harlem, or take a ferry for the awesome views of the famous skyline and the Statue of Liberty.

Grand Central Terminal
This Beaux Arts station has been a gateway to the city since 1913. Its concourse is a vast pedestrian area with an ornate, high-vaulted roof (see p54).

Statue of Liberty
The towering statue, a gift from France to the US in 1886, has become a symbol of freedom throughout the world (see pp12–13).

TENTH
NINTH
EIGHTH
CHELSI
Empire
Bu
GREENWICH
VILLAGE
WASHINGTON
SQUARE
WEST ST
VARICK
HOUSTON
SOHO
EAS
VILL
TRIBECA
BROADWAY
CANAL ST
BOWERY
LOWER
EAST SIDE
EAST BROADWAY
CIV M
CEN
LOWER
MANHATTAN
SOUTH
STREET VIADUCT
Brooklyn
Bridge
Hudson River

Ellis
Island

Statue of
Liberty

KEY

■ Major Sight

0 km   1

0 miles   1

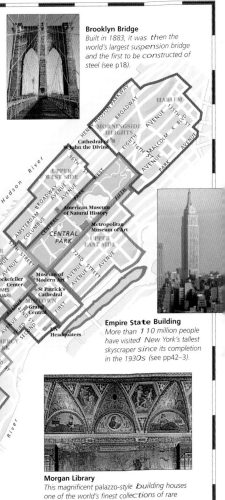

Brooklyn Bridge
Built in 1883, it was then the world's largest suspension bridge and the first to be constructed of steel (see p18).

Empire State Building
More than 110 million people have visited New York's tallest skyscraper since its completion in the 1930s (see pp42–3).

Morgan Library
This magnificent palazzo-style building houses one of the world's finest collections of rare manuscripts, prints, and books (see p57).

New York's Highlights

New York is a fantastic, energy-packed city. You can shop 'til you drop, eat from around the world, go to the theater, admire its stunning buildings, or take a stroll in many parks and squares. Getting around is easy on the subway, buses, and ferries.

Museums

American Museum of Natural History
One of the world's largest natural history museums exhibits everything from dinosaurs to Chinese costumes (see p69).

The Whitney Museum of American Art
The entire range of 20th-century American art can be seen in this collection. (see p69).

Metropolitan Museum of Art
The treasures of this mammoth museum includes a collection of more than 3,000 European paintings (see p69).

MoMA
This recently expanded museum has one of the world's most comprehensive collections of modern art, with works by Warhol and Picasso (see p61).

Solomon R. Guggenheim Museum
Housing one of the world's finest collections of modern and contemporary art, the shell-like museum is itself a masterpiece (see p69).

Architecture

Chrysler Building sparkles at night

Chrysler Building
The shimmering spire of this 77-story Art Deco building, resembling a car radiator grille, is one of New York's most loved landmarks (see p55).

Empire State Building
The tallest and most famous skyscraper in New York has attracted more than 110 million visitors since it opened in 1931 (see pp42–3).

Flatiron Building
In 1903, this wedge-shaped building, decorated in Italian Renaissance style, was renowned as the world's tallest (see p38).

Statue of Liberty
A symbol of freedom since its inauguration in 1886, this 305-ft (93-m) tall statue dominates New York's harbor (see pp12–13).

The Guggenheim's Great Rotunda

Grand Central Terminal

This builidng from 1913 is remarkable for its beauty. Of note is the vaulted ceiling of cerulean blue, decorated with twinkling stars (see p54).

Parks and Squares

Battery Park

Wedged between the water and a crush of buildings, this park is one of the best places in New York for gazing out to sea (see p15).

Central Park

With scenic hills, meadows, lakes, trees, and shrubs, this lush 843-acre (340-ha) park is an oasis of calm in the city's center and a great place to relax (see pp74–5).

The very private Gramercy Park

Gramercy Park

One of four squares laid out in the 1830s and 1840s, to attract smart society, today it is New York's only private park (see p39).

Madison Square

Once at the center of a fashionable residential area, it is now a pleasant place to stroll and admire statues of war heroes (see p38).

Sheridan Square

At the heart of Greenwich Village, where seven streets converge in such a maze that early guidebooks referred to the area as the "mousetrap" (see p30).

Multicult**u**ralism

Chinatow**n**

The shop**s** and sidewalk markets **o**verflow with exotic food**s**, herbs, and some unu**s**ual gifts. The area boasts an astounding 200 resta**u**rants (see p22).

Little Italy

The atmo**s**phere, colors, and flavor**s** of Italy still abound **i**n the area between Canal and Broome, **i**n its restaurants and coffee shops (see p22).

The Uppe**r** East Side

The ma**g**nificient St. Nicholas **R**ussian Orthodox Cathedra**l** is a reminder of the dispe**r**sed White Russian community (see p71).

The Lowe**r** East Side

Eldridge **S**treet Synagogue epitomi**z**es the religious traditions of this old Jewish area (see p22).

Harlem

Harlem, America's most famous black community is noted for its Renaissance writing, a**s** much as for its great go**s**pel entertainment and soul food. Harlem's famous **s**oul food restaurant is Sylvia's (see p85).

Gospel *singers* performing at Sylvia's *during* Sunday brunch

LOWER MANHATTAN

The old and new converge at Lower Manhattan, where early American monuments and Colonial churches stand in the shadow of skyscrapers. Commerce flourished after Man-a-hatt-ta island was bought from the Algonquians in 1626. Since 9/11, many buildings are still being repaired.

SIGHTS AT A GLANCE

Historic Buildings and Important Sites
Federal Reserve Bank ❶
Federal Hall ❷
New York Stock
　Exchange ❸
World Financial Center ❺
Fraunces Tavern Museum ❾

Museums
US Custom House ❼
Ellis Island ❸
Museum of
　Jewish
　Heritage ❶❺

Monuments and Statues
Statue of
　Liberty
　pp12–13
❶❷

Parks and Squares
Bowling
　Green
❻

Vietnam Veterans' Plaza ❶❶
Battery Park ❶❹

Boat Trips
Staten Island Ferry ❶❶

Churches
Trinity Church ❹
St. Elizabeth Ann Seton
　Shrine ❽

SEE ALSO

● *Street Life p15*

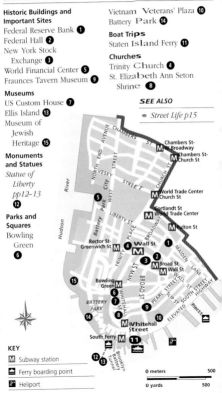

KEY

Ⓜ Subway station

🚢 Ferry boarding point

✈ Heliport

| 0 meters | 500 |
| 0 yards | 500 |

◀ *Trinity Church at the foot of Wall Street*

NY Stock Exchange tickertape machine, in use from 1870

Federal Reserve Bank ❶

Map 4H. Liberty St. Open Mon–Fri except public hols. Free.

This Italian-Renaissance style building is adorned with fine wrought-iron grillwork. Deep underground is a huge storehouse of gold, guarded by 90-ton doors. *The History of Money* exhibition, from 10am–4pm, has 800 items.

Federal Hall ❷

Map 4J. Wall St. Open Mon–Fri (Sat, Sun in Jul, Aug) except public hols. Free.

One of the city's finest Classical buildings, highlights

Federal Hall's columned rotunda

include the Bill of Rights Room and an interactive computer exhibit. George Washington's statue marks the spot where he took his oath of office in 1789.

New York Stock Exchange ❸

Map 4J. Broad St. Visitors' gallery not open.

Behind the Neo-Classical façade beats the financial heart of the US, grown from a local exchange to a global enterprise. Over 200 million shares are traded daily for more than 2,000 companies. Action on the trading floor is calmer now that everything is computerized.

Prominent early New Yorkers are buried in Trinity Church's graveyard

Trinity Church ❹

Map 4J. Broadway at Wall St. Open daily. Services Sun–Fri. Free.

This square-towered Episcopal church (1846), in one of the US's oldest Anglican parishes, was among the grandest Gothic Revival churches of its day. Highlights include sculpted brass doors and its 280-ft (86-m) steeple, New York's tallest structure until 1860.

World Financial Center ❺

Map 5H. West St. Free.

Top US financial companies have headquarters in this complex, damaged in the September 11 attack. At its heart is the dazzling Winter Garden, with a 120-ft (37-m) tall glass-and-steel atrium (all 2,000 panes of glass were replaced), palm trees, and 45 restaurants and shops, opening

Main floor of the Winter Garden's dazzling atrium

on to a lively piazza and marina on the Hudson River. The sweeping marble staircase leading down to the Winter Garden doubles as seating for free arts events.

Bowling Green ❻

Map 4J.

This triangular plot north of Battery Park was New York's first park, used as a cattle market, and then as a bowling ground. Beyond the Green, once surrounded by elegant homes, is the start of Broadway, running the length of Manhattan and, as Route 9, north to Albany, the State capital.

US Custom House ❼

Map 4J. Bowling Green. Museum open daily except Dec 25. Adm charge (free Thu).

The façade of this 1907 Beaux Arts granite palace has 44 Ionic columns, plus four heroic sculptures depicting the continents as seated women. Inside, murals decorate the fine marble rotunda. Since 1994, it has housed the Smithsonian National Museum of the American Indian, with a million artifacts and an archive of photographs, spanning the Americas' native cultures.

St. Elizabeth Ann Seton Shrine ❽

Map 4J. State St. Open Mon–Fri. Free.

Elizabeth Ann Seton (1774–1821), the first native-born American canonized by the Catholic Church, lived here in the early 1800s and founded the US's first order of nuns. The Mission, once a shelter for homeless Irish immigrant women, maintains her shrine.

Statue of Liberty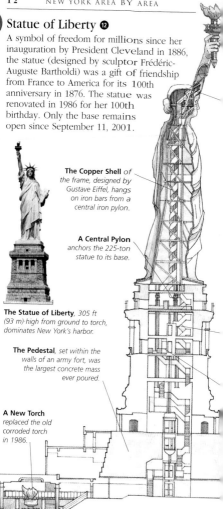

A symbol of freedom for millions since her inauguration by President Cleveland in 1886, the statue (designed by sculptor Frédéric-Auguste Bartholdi) was a gift of friendship from France to America for its 100th anniversary in 1876. The statue was renovated in 1986 for her 100th birthday. Only the base remains open since September 11, 2001.

The Copper Shell of the frame, designed by Gustave Eiffel, hangs on iron bars from a central iron pylon.

A Central Pylon anchors the 225-ton statue to its base.

The Statue of Liberty, 305 ft (93 m) high from ground to torch, dominates New York's harbor.

The Pedestal, set within the walls of an army fort, was the largest concrete mass ever poured.

A New Torch replaced the old corroded torch in 1986.

The Flame *of the replica torch is coated in 24-carat gold leaf.*

~ Crown

The Seven Rays *of Liberty's crown represent the seven seas and seven continents.*

Liberty Island *viewed from Castle Clinton National Monument.*

The Circle Line *ferry runs to the Statue of Liberty several times each day.*

~ **354 Steps** *lead from entrance to crown.*

~ Observation deck and museum

The Castle Clinton National Monument *at Battery Park is the departure point for Statue of Liberty–Ellis Island ferry.*

The 18th-century Fraunces Tavern Museum and restaurant

Fraunces Tavern Museum ❾

Map 4J. Pearl St. Open Tue–Sat except public hols & day after Thanksgiving. Free.

New York's only remaining block of 18th-century commercial buildings contains an exact replica of the 1719 Fraunces Tavern where George Washington said farewell to his officers in 1783. Its museum exhibits early American history.

Vietnam Veterans' Plaza ❿

Map 4J. Between Water St and South St.

In the center of a shopping plaza is a huge wall of translucent green glass, engraved with speeches, news stories, and moving letters to families from servicemen and women, who died in Vietnam.

Staten Island Ferry ⓫

Map 4J. Whitehall St. 24-hr service. Free.

The ferry has operated since 1810, carrying island commuters to and from the city. Visitors can get an unforgettable closeup of the Statue of Liberty and Manhattan's incredible skyline.

Staten Island Ferry is free – one of the city's best bargains

Statue of Liberty ⓬

See pp 12–13.

Ellis Island ⓭

Map 4J. Open daily except Dec 25. Adm charge: ferry fare gives entry to Ellis and Liberty Islands.

From 1892 to 1954, this symbol of America's immigrant

Over 600,000 names grace the Immigration Wall of Honor on Ellis Island

heritage was the arrival point for 12 million people seeking a better life. Today, their descendants (over 100 million) comprise almost 40 percent of the population. The museum's multimedia technology traces the immigrant experience.

Battery Park ⑭

Map 4J. Open daily.

Named for the cannons that once protected the harbor, the park, wedged between the water and the crush of buildings, is one of the city's best places for gazing out to sea. Its statues honor Jewish immigrants, the poet Emma Lazarus, the explorer Verrazano, and the Coast Guard.

Museum of Jewish Heritage ⑮

Map 5J. Battery Place. Open Sun–Fri, eve of Jewish holidays. Closed Sat, Jewish holidays, Thanksgiving. Adm charge.

With a core exhibition of over 2,000 photographs, 24 documentary films, and 800 artifacts about Jewish life, before, during, and after the Holocaust, it also has lectures, and performances, a memorial garden, a library, and a family history center.

Beaux Arts subway entrance at the corner of Battery Park

STREET LIFE

RESTAURANTS

Battery Garden
Map 4J. Battery Park, opposite 17 State.
Tel (212) 809 5508.
Moderate
New American menu with Asian accents.

Church & Dey
Map 4H. 55 Church St at Dey. Tel (212) 312 2000.
Moderate
Regional American classics with emphasis on seafood at restaurant in Millennium Hilton. Unobstructed view of World Trade Center site.

14 Wall Street
Map 4J. 14 Wall St, between New and Nassau.
Tel (212) 233 2780.
Moderate
A handsome setting for fine French cuisine. Service is impeccable and there's a convivial bar.

Fraunces Tavern
Map 4J. 54 Pearl St at Broad.
Tel (212) 968 1776.
Moderate
This recently opened 19th-century tavern, the former home of George Washington, features a charming restaurant.

Gigino's at Wagner Park
Map 5J. 20 Battery Place, next to the Museum of Jewish Heritage. Tel (212) 528 2228.
Moderate
Excellent Italian food from Amalfi coast. Sophisticated dining room and waterfront terrace have dazzling views.

See p96 for price codes.

SEAPORT AND
THE CIVIC CENTER

Manhattan's busy Civic Center is the hub of the city, state, and federal court systems. A handsome enclave of imposing architecture, its fine landmarks span periods from the 18th-century St. Paul's Chapel to the 20th-century Woolworth Building. The restored South Street Seaport is now home to restaurants, shops, and a museum. To the north is the magnificent Brooklyn Bridge.

SIGHTS AT A GLANCE

Historic Streets and Buildings
South Street Seaport **1**
Schermerhorn Row **2**
Brooklyn Bridge **3**
Criminal Courts Building **4**
Municipal Building **5**
Surrogate's Court, Hall of
    Records **6**
Woolworth Building **7**

Churches
St. Paul's Chapel **8**

SEE ALSO

• *Street Life p19*

KEY

M Subway station

Riverboat boarding point

◀ *South Street Seaport*

Fourth of July firework display over Brooklyn Bridge

South Street Seaport ❶

Map 3H. Fulton St. Museum (at Front St) open daily Apr–Oct, Fri–Sun in Nov–Mar except public hols. Adm charge.

The cobbled streets, piers, and buildings at the center of New York's 19th-century seafaring activity have been restored as a tourist center, with restaurants, food stalls, shops, a seafaring museum, and a fleet of tall ships.

Schermerhorn Row ❷

Map 4H. Fulton and South Sts.

This is the architectural showpiece of the seaport. Built as warehouses in 1811, this Row became desirable property when the Brooklyn Ferry terminus opened in 1814 and Fulton Market in 1822. Restored as part of the South Street development, it has 24 museum galleries, shops, and restaurants.

Fashionable Schermerhorn Row

Brooklyn Bridge ❸

Map 3H. Fulton and South Sts.

When it was completed in 1883, linking Manhattan and Brooklyn, this was the largest suspension bridge in the world and the first made of steel. Today, anyone walking across the 1-mile (1.8-km) span is rewarded with wonderful views of the city seen through the artistic wire cablework.

Criminal Courts Building ❹

Map 4H. Centre St. Open Mon–Fri except public hols. Free.

The three-story-high entrance of this 1939 Art Moderne building, with towers like a Babylonian temple's, is set behind two huge, square, free-standing granite columns. An aerial walkway links the courts with the correctional center across the street.

Municipal Building ❺

Map 4H. Centre St. Free.

Built in 1914, this 25-story structure, dominating the Civic Center and straddling Chambers Street, was McKim, Mead, and White's first "skyscraper." It houses government offices and a marriage chapel. The top, a fantasy of towers capped by Adolph Wienman's statue *Civic Fame*, is its most notable feature.

Surrogate's Court, Hall of Records ❻

Map 4H. Chambers St. Only lobby open during renovations except public hols. Free.

An interior inspired by the Paris Opéra is one of the glories of this 1911 Beaux Arts beauty, boasting a magnificent central hall with marble stairways and ceiling mosaics. The ornate façade features statues representing the seasons, commerce, Justice, and notable New Yorkers. The Hall of Records holds public records dating as far back as 1664.

Fantasy façade of the Municipal Building

Woolworth Building ❼

Map 4H. Broadway. Free.

This 1913 skyscraper is topped by a pyramid roof, flying buttresses, pinnacles, and four small towers. Inside, bronze filigree, stained glass, marble walls, and a mosaic ceiling, are magical. The lobby has a bas-relief caricature of the owner.

St. Paul's Chapel ❽

Map 4H. Broadway. Open daily except public hols. Free.

This Georgian gem is Manhattan's only remaining church built before the Revolutionary War. The colorful interior is lit by ornate crystal chandeliers.

STREET LIFE

RESTAURANTS

Bridge Café
Map 4H. 279 Water St at Dover St. Tel (212) 227 3344.
Moderate
Surprisingly sophisticated American menu.

Cabana at the Seaport
Map 3H. Pier 17, 3rd level, South Street Seaport. Tel (212) 406 1155.
Moderate
Cuban-Caribbean menu.

Harbor Lights
Map 3H. Pier 17, 3rd level, South Street Seaport. Tel (212) 227 2800.
Moderate
Steak and seafood.

Quartino
Map 3H. 21–23 Peck Slip. Tel (212) 349 4433.
Moderate
Convivial Italian wine bar.

Red
Map 3H. 19 Fulton St, between Front & Water Sts. Tel (212) 571 5900.
Cheap
Colorful Tex-Mex spot.

Sequoia
Map 3H. Pier 17, South Street Seaport. Tel (212) 732 9090.
Moderate
Nautical décor, seafood menu, and breathtaking views.

See p96 for price codes.

LOWER EAST SIDE

Nowhere does the strong ethnic flavor of New York come through more tangibly than in Lower Manhattan, where immigrants began to settle in the late 1800s. Italians, Chinese, and Jews established distinct neighborhoods, preserving their languages, customs, foods, and religions in a strange land. The area brims with restaurants, with a spirit found nowhere else.

SIGHTS AT A GLANCE

Historic Streets and Buildings
Police Headquarters
  Building ❶
Little Italy ❷
Chinatown ❸
Puck Building ❻
Engine Company No. 31 ❼

Museums
Lower East Side Tenement
  Museum ❺

Synagogues
Eldridge Street Synagogue ❹

SEE ALSO

• *Street Life p23*

KEY

Ⓜ Subway station

| 0 meters | 500 |
| 0 yards | 500 |

◀ Dragon puppet in Chinatown at Chinese New Year

Police Headquarters Building ❶

Map 4G. Centre St. Closed to the public.

From 1909–73, the city's police department was housed in this monumental, columned Baroque building, in a wedge-shaped site near Little Italy. Its ornate dome dominates the skyline and can be seen from City Hall. In 1985, it was converted into luxury apartments.

Little Italy ❷

Map 4G. Streets around Mulberry St.

The community that grew up around Mulberry Street was lively with the colors, flavors, and atmosphere of Italy. Now a smaller area between Canal and Broome remains strictly Italian, filled with restaurants offering simple, rustic food, coffee shops with tempting pastries, and chic boutiques.

Chinatown ❸

Map 4G. Streets around Mott St. Eastern States Buddhist Temple open daily. Free.

More than 200,000 Chinese live in Chinatown. The shops and sidewalk markets overflow with exotic foods

A Chinese grocer on Canal Street

and herbs, gifts from fine antiques to backscratchers, and an astounding 200 restaurants. For a different experience, step inside the incense-scented Buddhist Temple on Mott Street.

Eldridge Street Synagogue's lavishly decorated façade

Eldridge Street Synagogue ❹

Map 3G. Eldridge St. Open Tue–Sun. Adm charge.

The impressive façade of this flamboyant 1887 temple has Romanesque, Gothic, and Moorish touches. Inside, the hand-carved ark, sculpted wooden balcony, brass chandeliers, stained glass, and marbleized wood paneling show why this building was the pride of the area. Closed since the 1930s, it is being restored.

Lower East Side Tenement Museum ❺

Map 3G. Orchard St. Guided tours only (book ahead) Tue–Sun except public hols. Adm charge.

Guided tours inside this tenement building give an

insight into the deplorable conditions in which people lived: a German-Jewish seamstress in 1874, orthodox Jews from Lithuania in 1918, and Sicilian Catholics during the 1930s. Many rooms had no windows, and indoor plumbing was rare.

Puck Building ⑥

Map 4F. Lafayette St. Open during business hours. Free.

The horizontal bands of arched windows and molded red brick of this block-square architectural curiosity of 1885 reveals its mid-1800s German design influence. In 1900, it was the world's largest building devoted to lithography and publishing and, until 1916, was home to satirical magazine *Puck*.

Engine Company's French façade

Engine Company No. 31 ⑦

Map 4G. Lafayette St. Closed to the public.

Memorable architecture in its day, this 1895 fire station resembles a Loire château, with its steep roof, dormers, and towers, which seem almost fairy tale-like in today's location. It now houses the Downtown Community Television Center, with courses and workshops for its members.

STREET LIFE

RESTAURANTS

Katz's Delicatessen
Map 3F. 205 East Houston St at Ludlow. Tel (212) 254 2246.
Cheap
Try the pastrami on rye.

Ratmer's/Lansky Lounge
Map 3F. 138 Delancey St at Norfolk
Tel (212) 677 5588/9489.
Cheap/Moderate
Blintzes by day/steak at night.

Sammy's Roumanian
Map 3G. 157 Chrystie St.
Tel (212) 673 0330. **Moderate**
Chopped liver and schmaltz.

WD-50
Map 3F. 50 Clinton St between Rivington & Stanton.
Tel (212) 477 2900. **Moderate**
Hip café famous for its food.

SHOPPING

Fine & Klein
Map 3F. 119 Orchard St.
High-quality handbags and accessories, at a discount.

Fishkin's Knitwear
Map 3G. 314 Grand St at Allen.
Discount clothing and shoes.

Forman's
Map 3G. 78, 82, and 94 Orchard St.
Brand names, discount prices.

Giselle Sportswear
Map 3F. 143 Orchard St.
Discount designer clothing.

Harry Zarin Fabric Warehouse
Map 3G. 318 Grand St.
Wholesale fabrics, upholstery. See p96 for price codes.

SOHO AND TRIBECA

Art and architecture are the twin lures that transformed these former industrial districts. Its rare cast-iron architecture saved from demolition in the 1960s, SoHo (south of Houston) today is the place for brunch and gallery hopping, while trendy TriBeCa (triangle below Canal) attracts the latest galleries and newest restaurants.

SIGHTS AT A GLANCE

Historic Streets and Buildings
Greene Street ❶
Singer Building ❷
White Street ❻

Museums and Galleries
New Museum of
    Contemporary Art ❸

New York Earth Room ❹
New York City Fire
    Museum ❺

SEE ALSO

• *Street Life p27*

◀ Cast-iron façades on Greene Street

Richard Haas mural on Greene St

Greene Street **1**

Map 4G.

Cast-iron architecture flourished in New York in the 1800s, producing decorative elements such as arches and columns, to create cheap but impressive buildings. Greene Street (between Canal and Grand, Broome, and Spring Streets) has 50 of these beauties.

Singer Building **2**

Map 4F. Broadway. Free.

By 1900, cast iron was giving way to steel-framed brick and terracotta. A notable example is this charmingly ornate, 12-story Singer Building, adorned with wrought-iron balconies and graceful arches painted a striking dark green.

New Museum of Contemporary Art **3**

Map 4F. Broadway. Open Tue–Sat. Temporary address: Chelsea Art Museum, West 22nd St at 11th Ave. Adm charge.

Marcia Tucker founded this museum in 1977. Jeff Koons

and the late John Cage are among the artists featured in thematic shows. The Media Lounge explores digital art, video installations, and sound works. It will move to the Bowery in 2007.

New York Earth Room **4**

Map 4F. Wooster St. Open Wed–Sat. Free.

Of the three Earth Rooms created by conceptual artist Walter De Maria, this is the only one still in existence. Commissioned by the Dia Art Foundation in 1977, the interior earth sculpture consists of 280,000 lbs (127,000 kg) of dirt piled 22 in (56 cm) deep in a 3,600-sq ft (335-sq m) room.

La France 1901 horse-drawn steam pumper in the City Fire Museum

New York City Fire Museum **5**

Map 5G. Spring St. Open Tue–Sun except public hols. Adm charge.

This splendid museum is housed in a Beaux Arts (1904) firehouse. The city's unsurpassed collection of fire-fighting equipment and memorabilia, from the 1700s to 1917, includes scale models, bells, and hydrants. Upstairs, fire engines are neatly lined up for an 1890 parade. An interactive fire simulation, available for groups, gives an insight into fire fighting in New York.

White Street ⑥

Map 4G.

This sampling of TriBeCa cast-iron architecture shows a wide range of styles. No. 2 has Federal features and a rare gambrel roof. Nos. 8 to 10 sport impressive Tuscan columns and arches, their Neo-Renaissance style of shorter upper stories giving an

Rudi Stern's Let There Be Neon gallery in White Street

illusion of height. In contrast, No. 38 houses neon artist Rudi Stern's gallery, Let There Be Neon.

STREET LIFE

RESTAURANTS

Bouley Bakery
Map 4G. 120 West Broadway at Duane.
Tel (212) 964 2525.
Moderate
David Bouley's New French cuisine is heavenly.

Danube
Map 5G. 30 Hudson St, between Duane and Reade.
Tel (212) 791 3771.
Expensive
Nouveau Austrian food.

The Odeon
Map 4H. 145 Broadway at Thomas. Tel (212) 233 0507.
Moderate
Art Deco décor, good food, and a star-studded crowd.

Le Zinc
Map 4H. 139 Duane St, between Church and West Broadway. Tel (212) 513 0001.
Moderate
Welcoming, informal bistro.

BARS AND LOUNGES

Double Happiness
Map 4G. 173 Mott St at Broome.
Cavernous bar, mixing China and Italy.

N
Map 4G. 33 Crosby St, between Broome and Grand.
Raffish bar with Spanish tapas and flamenco music.

NIGHTLIFE

Church Lounge
Map 4G. TriBeCa Grand Hotel, 2 Sixth Ave.
Plush seats and a dramatic, eight-story atrium.

Liquor Store Bar
Map 4G. 235 West Broadway at White.
Comfortable place for a beer.

The Screening Room
Map 4G. 54 Varick St at Laight.
Ultimate movie date. Chic bistro dining, then a film.

See p96 for price codes.

GREENWICH VILLAGE

New Yorkers call it "the Village." The crazy-quilt pattern of streets makes it a natural enclave that has been a bohemian haven and home to many celebrated artists and writers. Today, it is also a popular gay district. The area has become mainstream and expensive, overwhelmed with smart boutiques and trendy restaurants.

SIGHTS AT A GLANCE

Historic Streets and Buildings
St. Luke's Place ❶
Jefferson Market
    Courthouse ❸
Patchin Place ❹

Galleries
Forbes Magazine Building ❺

Churches
Church of the Ascension ❻
Judson Memorial Church ❼

Squares
Sheridan Square ❷

SEE ALSO

• *Street Life p31*

KEY

Ⓜ Subway station

◀ *Billboards at corner of Christopher Street and Seventh Avenue South*

St. Luke's Place ❶

Map 5F.

Fifteen elegant, Italianate 1850s row houses line the north side. *Wait Until Dark* was filmed at No. 4; the tall lamps at No. 6 signify it was a former mayor's home; No. 10 was the Huxtables family home in *The Cosby Show*; Theodore Dreiser wrote *An American Tragedy* at No. 16; and poet Marianne Moore also lived here.

Elegant façades and an ailanthus tree add to Patchin Place's beauty

Sheridan Square ❷

Map 5F.

This is the heart of the Village, where seven streets converge. In 1863, the Draft Riots took place here. A century later, another famous disturbance rocked the square, at the Stonewall Inn on Christopher Street, resulting in a landmark moral victory for the new Gay Rights movement.

Patchin Place ❹

Map 5E. West 10th St.

This tiny, tree-lined block of mid-1800s houses is one of the Village's many delightful pockets; they later became fashionable. Many writers lived here: poets e e cummings and John Masefield, playwright Eugene O'Neill, and John Reed, whose account of the Russian Revolution was made into the film *Reds*.

Jefferson Market Courthouse ❸

Map 5E. Ave. of the Americas. Open Mon–Sat except public hols. Free.

This treasured Village landmark (now a public library), with its Venetian Gothic-style turrets and spires, stained glass, spiral staircase, and four-sided clock, was voted one of America's ten most beautiful buildings when it opened in 1877.

Statue, Christopher Park

Forbes Magazine Building ❺

Map 4E. 5th Ave. Galleries open Tue–Wed, (groups only Thu), Fri–Sat except public hols. Free.

The Forbes Magazine Galleries, housed in a 1925 limestone cube, show the late Malcolm Forbes's diverse tastes. Among the historical memorabilia are 500 antique toy boats, 12,000 toy soldiers, trophies, monopoly games, and a signed copy of Lincoln's Gettysburg Address. Paintings, from French to American military works, are also on display.

Church of the Ascension 6

Map 4E. 5th Ave at 10th St. Open daily. Free.

This English Gothic Revival church was designed in 1840–41 by Richard Upjohn, architect of Trinity Church. The interior was redone in 1888 by Stanford White, with an altar relief by Augustus Saint-Gaudens. Above the altar hangs *The Ascension*, a mural by John La Farge, who also designed some of the stained glass.

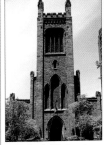

Gothic Church of the Ascension

La Farge, the church was built in 1892 as a memorial to Adoniram Judson, the first American Baptist missionary in Asia; his Bible was placed in the cornerstone at the dedication. White's use of mottled yellow brick and white terracotta trim introduced light coloration into American church architecture.

Judson Memorial Church 7

Map 4F. Washington Square South. Open Sun–Fri. Free.

An elegant Romanesque work by Stanford White, with stained glass by John

STREET LIFE

RESTAURANTS

Blue Hill

Map 4F. 75 Washington Place at MacDougal. Tel (212) 539 1776.
Moderate
Highly praised New American fare that uses local, seasonal ingredients, served in intimate, elegant surroundings.

Blue Ribbon Bakery

Map 4F. 33 Downing St at Bedford. Tel (212) 337 0404.
Moderate
A casual Village favorite with an enormous, eclectic menu that includes everything from croissants and caviar to the signature fried chicken.

Café Loup

Map 5E. 105 West 13th St. Tel (212) 255 4746.
Moderate
An agreeable French bistro, with tuna carpaccio, roast chicken, and steak. Romantic setting and funky bar.

Da Silvano

Map 5F. 260 Sixth Ave, between Bleecker and West Houston. Tel (212) 982 2343.
Moderate
Great place for celebrity watching. Northern Italian fare here is consistent.

See p96 for price codes.

EAST VILLAGE

Peter Stuyvesant had a country estate in the East Village, but around 1900 Germans, Jews, Poles, Ukrainians, Puerto Ricans, and the Irish arrived, leaving their cultural marks in ethnic restaurants and churches. In the 1950s, the "beat generation," followed by hippies and punks, moved in. Their experimental music clubs and theaters still abound. The once seedy "Alphabet City" has now become one of New York's trendiest areas.

SIGHTS AT A GLANCE

Historic Streets and Buildings
Cooper Union **1**
Colonnade Row **3**
Bayard-Condict Building **7**

Museums
Merchant's House
Museum **4**

Churches
St. Mark's-in-the-Bowery
Church **5**
Grace Church **6**

Famous Theaters
Public Theater **2**

SEE ALSO

• *Street Life p35*

KEY
M Subway station

◀ *The interior of McSorley's Old Ale House on East Seventh Street*

Cooper Union opened in 1859

Cooper Union ❶

Map 4E. East 7th St. Open
Mon–Sat except Jun–Aug,
public hols. Free.

Founded by self-made man
Peter Cooper in 1859, this
six-story building, the first to
be made with a steel frame,
was New York's first free,
nonsectarian coeducational
college, specializing in
design, architecture, and
engineering. Mark Twain
inaugurated the Great Hall;
in 1860, Lincoln made his
"Right makes Might" speech.

Public Theater ❷

Map 4F. Lafayette St.

This large redbrick and
brownstone, German
Romanesque Revival
building was the Astor
Library in 1849. The
late Joseph Papp,
in 1965, persuaded
the city to buy it as
a home for his
Shakespeare company
(now the Public
Theater). Its 1967
renovation preserved
much of the hand-
some interior during
its conversion into
six impressive theaters.

Colonnade Row ❸

Map 4F. Lafayette St.
Closed to the public.

The Corinthian columns
across these four buildings
are all that remain of a once-
magnificent row of nine
Greek Revival town houses.
Cornelius Vanderbilt and
John Jacob Astor once lived
here, as did Washington
Irving, of *Rip Van Winkle*
fame, and English novelists
Charles Dickens and William
Makepeace Thackeray.

Merchant's House Museum ❹

Map 4F. East 4th St. Open
Mon–Thu by appt. Adm charge.

This remarkable 1832 Greek
Revival brick town house,
tucked away on an East
Village block, is a time
capsule of a vanished way
of life. It still has its original
fixtures and fittings, and is
filled with the actual furniture, ornaments, and uten-
sils of the Tredwell family,
who lived here for 100
years. The very grand first-
floor parlors show how the
wealthy lived in the 1800s.

*The original 19th-century iron stove in the
kitchen of the Merchant's House Museum*

St. Mark's-in-the-Bowery Church ❺

Map 4E. East 10th St. Open Sun–Fri. Free.

New York's second oldest church, built in 1799, stands on land that was once a farm; its steeple was added in 1828. Poet W. H. Auden, who was a parishioner, is commemorated here. The politically committed 1960s congregation continues to be avant-garde.

Grace Church ❻

Map 4E. Broadway. Open Sun for services. Free.

This beautiful 1846 masterpiece, with its delicate early Gothic lines, is a calm respite in the Village. The elegant interior has Pre-Raphaelite stained glass and a handsome mosaic floor.

Bayard-Condict Building ❼

Map 4F. Bleecker St. Free.

The graceful columns, elegant filigreed terra-cotta façade, and magnificent cornice on this 1898 building mark the only New York work by Louis Sullivan, the great Chicago architect.

Grace Church altar and window

STREET LIFE

RESTAURANTS

Daily Chow

Map 3F. 2 East 2nd St at the Bowery. Tel (212) 254 7887.
Cheap
Pan-Asian specialties.

First

Map 3F. 87 1st Ave, between 5th & 6th Sts.
Tel (212) 674 3823.
Moderate
Creative continental dishes. Sunday Sopranos special.

Jeollado

Map 3F. 116 East 4th St at 1st Ave. Tel (212) 260 7696.
Moderate
Imaginative Japanese sushi or Korean pancakes.

Teresa's

Map 3F. 103 1st Ave, between 6th & 7th Sts.
Tel (212) 228 0604.
Cheap
Polish comfort food guaranteed to fill you up without emptying your pockets. The pierogis and potato pancakes are perfection.

Veselka

Map 3E. 144 2nd Ave at 9th St. Tel (212) 228 9682.
Cheap
A funky Ukrainian diner serving borscht, blintzes, and pierogis for a pittance. Tables at the back are quieter.

See p96 for price codes.

GRAMERCY AND THE FLATIRON DISTRICT

Four squares were laid out in this area by developers in the 1800s to emulate the quiet, residential areas in many European cities. Gramercy Park, still mainly residential, was one of them. Its townhouses, designed by some of the city's best architects, were home to many prominent citizens. Chic boutiques and cafés now occupy a once-dowdy area south of the Flatiron Building.

SIGHTS AT A GLANCE

Historic Streets and Buildings
Appellate Division of the Supreme Court of the State of New York 2
Metropolitan Life Insurance Company 3
Flatiron Building 4
Block Beautiful 7
Gramercy Park Hotel 8

Museums
Theodore Roosevelt Birthplace 5

Parks and Squares
Madison Square 1
Gramercy Park 6

SEE ALSO

• Street Life p39

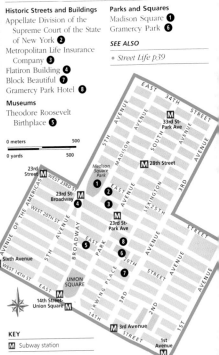

KEY

M Subway station

◄ Con Edison headquarters by night

Madison Square ❶

Map 4D.

This fashionable, residential square of 1847 sported the Fifth Avenue Hotel, the Madison Square Theater, and the original Madison Square Garden. Later office development brought the distinguished Metropolitan Life and Flatiron buildings. Today, it's a pleasant place to stroll and admire the statues of war heroes.

Statues of Justice and Study stand on Appellate Court's roof

Appellate Division of the Supreme Court of the State of New York ❷

Map 4D. East 25th St at Madison Ave. Open Mon–Fri except public hols. Free.

Appeals relating to criminal and civil cases for New York and the Bronx are heard here. This small, marble, Palladian Revival building of 1900 is decorated with handsome sculptures. Its elegant interior has stained-glass windows, murals, and cabinetwork. The lobby features some famous cases.

Metropolitan Life Insurance Company ❸

Map 4D. Madison Ave. Open banking hours. Free.

In 1909, a 700-ft (210-m) tower, added to the 54-story edifice, ousted the Flatiron as the world's tallest building. The minute hands of its four-sided clock each weigh 1,000 lb (454 kg). Lit up at night, the building served as the company symbol: "the light that never fails."

Flatiron Building ❹

Map 4D. 5th Ave. Open office hours. Free.

Dwarfed by taller structures today, in 1903 this striking building was the world's tallest. One of the first to use a steel frame, it heralded the era of the skyscrapers. The Italian Renaissance decoration is mostly in terra-cotta. Its slim, rounded façade is as proud as a ship's prow sailing up the avenue.

Flatiron Building, at the triangle of Fifth Ave, Broadway, and 23rd St

Theodore Roosevelt Birthplace **5**

Map 4D. East 20th St. Open Tue–Sat except public hols. Adm charge.

The reconstructed boyhood home of the colorful 26th president shows everything from campaign buttons and toys to a "Rough Rider" hat.

Gramercy Park **6**

Map 4D.

One of four squares (with Stuyvesant, Madison, and Union) laid out in the 1800s, it is the city's only private park, with fine buildings and graceful cast-iron gates.

Block Beautiful **7**

Map 4E. East 19th St.

This is a serene, tree-lined block of 1920s residences, beautifully restored. None of them is outstanding on its

Façade of a Block Beautiful house

own, but together they create a wonderfully harmonious whole.

Gramercy Park Hotel **8**

Map 4D. Lexington Ave at 21st.

For more than 60 years, this shabbily chic hotel, with antique sconces and wood-slat windows in the delightful, old-fashioned bar, drew all types. It reopens in 2007.

STREET LIFE

RESTAURANTS

11 Madison Park
Map 4D. Madison Ave at East 24th St. Tel (212) 889 0905.
Moderate
New American cuisine. Chic, elegant Art Deco setting.

Gramercy Tavern
Map 4E. 42 East 20th St at Broadway.
Tel (212) 477 0777.
Moderate
Inventive American cuisine.

Kitchen 22
Map 4D. 36 East 22nd St.
Tel (212) 228 4399. **Moderate**
A bargain, prix-fixé menu in a stylish venue.

Tabla and Tabla Bread Bar
Map 4D. 11 Madison Ave at East 25th St.
Tel (212) 889 0667.
Moderate
New American with Indian seasonings, served in colorful surroundings.

Veritas
Map 4E. 43 East 20th St, between Broadway and Park Ave South.
Tel (212) 353 3700.
Expensive
An amazing wine list. The New American cuisine is also outstanding. Reserve ahead.

See p96 for price codes.

CHELSEA AND
THE GARMENT DISTRICT

Once open farmland, this area had become commercial by the 1870s. Music halls lined 23rd Street. Fashion Row flourished, with department stores for middle-class New York; the garment district grew up around Macy's. Today, Chelsea is filled with art galleries and antique shops.

SIGHTS AT A GLANCE

Historic Streets and Buildings
Empire State Building
pp42–3 **2**
General Post Office **6**

Churches
Marble Collegiate Reformed
Church **1**
St. John the Baptist
Church **4**

Modern Architecture
Madison Square Garden **5**
Chelsea Piers Complex **7**

Monuments
Worth Monument **9**

Landmark Hotels
Chelsea Hotel **8**

Landmark Stores
Macy's **3**

SEE ALSO

• Street Life p45

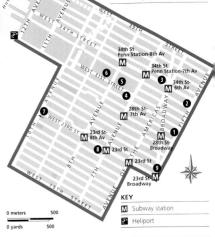

KEY

M	Subway station
⊞	Heliport

0 meters 500
0 yards 500

◀ Inside Chelsea's Empire Diner

Empire State Building ❷

The Empire State Building is the tallest and most famous skyscraper in New York. More than 110 million visitors have gazed down on the city from the Observatory since it opened in 1931. This elegant Art Deco classic has been featured in countless movies, such as *King Kong*.

The Empire State Building *dominates the New York skyline.*

Colored Floodlighting *of the top 30 floors marks special and seasonal events.*

The Framework *is made from 60,000 tons of steel and was built in 23 weeks.*

Aluminum panels around the 6,500 windows

Ten Million Bricks *were used to line the whole building.*

Entrance *from Fifth Avenue.*

102nd-floor observatory

The Empire State was planned to be 86 stories high, then a mooring mast was added. Now 204 ft (62 m) high, it transmits TV and radio to the city and four states.

High-speed Elevators travel at up to 1,200 ft (366 m) a minute.

Symbols of the Modern Age are depicted on these bronze Art Deco medallions placed in the lobby.

Outdoor Observation Decks on the 86th Floor provide bird's-eye views of Manhattan. The 102nd floor, at 1,250 ft (381 m) high, has been closed to the public for several years.

The Fifth Avenue Marble-lined Entrance Lobby has a relief image of the skyscraper super-imposed on a map of New York State.

Over 200 Steel and concrete piles support the 365,000-ton building.

VISITORS' CHECKLIST

Map 4C. 5th Ave.
Tel (212) 736 3100. 86th-floor Observatory open daily:
9:30am to midnight (9am to 5pm Dec 24, 11am to 7pm Dec 25, Jan 1). Audio guides available. Wheelchair access. Restaurant. Adm charge.
www.esbnyc.com

Marble Collegiate Reformed Church ❶

Map 4D. West 29th St. Open daily except public hols. Free.

Best known for its former pastor Norman Vincent Peale, this church was built in 1854 from marble blocks. Inside, its walls have a stenciled gold *fleur-de-lis* design on a soft rust background. Tiffany stained-glass windows were added in 1893.

Empire State Building ❷

See pp42–3.

Macy's ❸

Map 5C. West 34th St. Open daily except public hols.

The "world's largest store" covers a square block, and inside you can buy just about anything in every price range. The red star logo was from the owner's tattoo, a souvenir of his sailing days. The 34th Street façade has its original caryatids guarding the entrance, along with the clock, canopy, and lettering.

At Macy's you can buy anything you want – from food to futons

St. John the Baptist Church ❹

Map 5D. West 31st St. Open daily.

The sanctuary of this plain-façaded, single-spired, Roman Catholic church (1840) is a marvel of Gothic arches in glowing white marble surmounted by gilded capitals. Painted reliefs of religious scenes, set off by stained-glass windows, line the walls. Its peaceful Prayer Garden has religious statuary, stone benches, and a fountain.

The marvelous Gothic interior of St. John the Baptist Church

Madison Square Garden ❺

Map 5C. Pennsylvania Plaza. Open daily. Adm charge.

Home to the "Knicks" basketball, New York Rangers hockey, and Liberty (women's) basketball teams, the 20,000-seat Garden is also used for rock concerts, ice shows, dog shows, wrestling, tennis, boxing, and the circus. There is a 5,600-seat theater as well.

A 280-ft (85-m) inscription runs across the full length of the Post Office

General Post Office ⑥

Map 5D. 8th Ave. Open 24 hrs a day including public hols.

This imposing, two-block-long, Beaux Arts structure of 1913 has a broad staircase leading to a façade, with 20 Corinthian columns and a pavilion at each end.

Chelsea Piers Complex ⑦

Map 6E. 11th Ave (17th to 23rd Sts). Open daily. Adm charge.

This huge 1995 complex has skating rinks, a golf-driving range, running tracks, a marina, and 11 TV and film production sound stages.

Chelsea Hotel ⑧

Map 5D. West 23rd St.

The hotel has always drawn musicians, writers, and artists, such as Jack Kerouac, Tennessee Williams, Mark Twain, and Dylan Thomas. Soak up the bar's decadent, creative atmosphere.

Worth Monument ⑨

Map 4D. 5th Ave and Broadway.

A cast-iron fence of swords surrounds this 1857 obelisk honoring General Worth, a hero of the Mexican wars. He is the only public figure buried under Manhattan.

STREET LIFE

RESTAURANTS

Chelsea Bistro & Bar
Map 5D. 358 West 23rd St, between 8th and 9th Aves. Tel (212) 727 2026.
Moderate
Romantic Paris in Chelsea.

Da Umberto
Map 5E. 107 West 17th St, between 6th and 7th Aves. Tel (212) 989 0303.
Moderate
Sophisticated Tuscan fare.

Empire Diner
Map 5E. 210 10th Ave. Tel (212) 243 2736.
Cheap
Art Deco beauty.

Le Madri
Map 5E. 168 West 18th St at 7th Ave. Tel (212) 727 8022.
Moderate
Northern Italian cookery.

The Red Cat
Map 5D. 227 10th Ave, between 23rd and 24th Sts. Tel (212) 242 1122.
Moderate
First-rate American fare.

BARS

Chelsea Brewing Co
Map 6E. Pier 59, 11th Ave.
Large, fun-filled brewpub.

See p96 for price codes.

Hudson River

THEATER DISTRICT

The Metropolitan Opera House's move to Broadway in 1883 drew lavish theaters and restaurants to the area. In the 1920s, movie palaces added neon glamor to Broadway (the "Great White Way"). The glitter faded, but redevelopment has brought the bright lights back.

SIGHTS AT A GLANCE

Historic Streets and Buildings
New York Public Library **6**
Times Square **8**
Group Health Insurance
Building **10**
Shubert Alley **11**

Museums and Galleries
International Center of
Photography **7**
Intrepid Sea-Air-Space
Museum **14**

Modern Architecture
Rockefeller Center **1**

Famous Theaters
Lyceum Theater **3**
New Amsterdam Theater **9**

City Center of Music and
Dance **12**
Carnegie Hall **13**

Landmark Hotels
Algonquin Hotel **4**
Bryant Park Hotel **5**

Landmark Stores
Diamond Row **2**

SEE ALSO

• *Street Life* p51

```
0 meters    500
0 yards     500
```

KEY

M Subway station

Riverboat boarding point

◀ *The heart of the Theater District, around Times Square*

Rockefeller Center, looking toward the General Electric Building

Rockefeller Center **1**

Map 4B. NBC, Rockefeller Center, Radio City Music Hall open daily. Guided tours. Free.

With 19 buildings (five modern and 14 original Art Deco), this is the largest privately owned complex in the world. Begun in the 1930s, Rockefeller Center was the first commercial project to integrate gardens, dining, and shopping with office space. Over 100 works of art are on public display, including a major mural in each building.

Diamond Row **2**

Map 4B. 47th St between 5th and 6th Aves.

Jewelry glitters in every window of this block, the center of New York's wholesale and retail trade that handles 80 percent of the diamonds coming into the US. It began in the 1930s when Jewish

diamond cutters fled from Antwerp and Amsterdam to escape Nazism. Above the stores are workshops where the stones are cut and set.

Lyceum Theater **3**

Map 5B. West 45th St.

The oldest New York theater still active, this extravagant Baroque-style bandbox as frilly as a wedding cake, dates from 1903. It made history with a record run of 1,600 performances of *Born Yesterday* and was the first theater to be designated a historic landmark.

The Rose Room, Algonquin Hotel

Algonquin Hotel **4**

Map 5C. West 44th St.

A literary landmark, famous for the *New Yorker* "Round Table" that included Dorothy Parker, Robert Benchley, Alexander Woollcott, and Harold Ross, the Algonquin remains an oasis of civility, with antique lighting fixtures and cartoon wallpaper. The charming, elegant Rose Room or the cozy, paneled lobby is a good place to meet.

Bryant Park Hotel ➎

Map 5C. West 40th St.

Formerly the American Radiator building, the sleek 1924 design is illusory, making it seem taller than its 23 stories. The black brick façade is set off by gold terra-cotta trim, evoking images of flaming coals. This luxury hotel features the New York outpost of the trendy LA eatery, Koi.

The New York Public Library ➏

Map 4C. 5th Ave and 42nd St. Open Tue–Sun except public hols. Free.

The epitome of Beaux Arts elegance, this white marble 1911 landmark is stunning both inside and out. Its many magnificent features include vaulted marble halls, imposing stairways, terraces, and fountains. The cathedral-like, paneled Main Reading Room stretches for two full blocks and glows with suffused light from its great arched windows.

Gold-trimmed Bryant Park Hotel

International Center of Photography ➐

Map 5C. Ave of the Americas and 43rd St. Open Tue–Sun except Jul 4. Free.

Cornell Capa founded the center in 1974 to conserve the work of photojournalists like his brother Robert, killed on assignment in 1954. The 12,500 original prints are by many top photographers, including Ansel Adams and Henri Cartier-Bresson. Exhibitions, films, lectures, and classes take place regularly.

Times Square ➑

Map 5C.

Called the "Crossroads of the World," it is New York's most famous intersection, the symbol of the nearby theater district that includes Broadway. In 1904, the *New York Times* built a 25-story tower and renamed the site. Since the 1990s, new offices, theaters, and shops have transformed the area.

Entrance to the New York Public Library's Main Reading Room

New Amsterdam Theater ❾

Map 5C. West 42nd St.
Guided tours Thu–Tue.

This was America's most opulent theater when it opened in 1903, and the first to have an Art Nouveau interior. Florenz Ziegfeld produced his famous *Follies* here from 1914 to 1918, with Broadway's first $5 ticket price. Restored by Disney, it is now home to the popular *The Lion King*.

Group Health Insurance Building ❿

Map 5C. West 42nd St. Open office hours. Free.

This unusual 1931 building has a stepped profile seen from east and west, but a slab effect from north or south. Its nickname of "jolly green giant" comes from the exterior's horizontal bands of blue-green terra-cotta. Inside is a classic Art Deco lobby of opaque glass and stainless steel.

Shubert Alley ⓫

Map 5C. Between West 44th and West 45th Sts.

West of Broadway the playhouses are rich in theater lore and notable architecture. Two classic 1913 theaters – Booth (222 West 45th Street) and Shubert (225 West 44th) – form the west wall of Shubert Alley. Across from the 44th Street end of the alley is St. James, where *Oklahoma!* and *The King and I* played.

The tiled Moorish façade of the City Center of Music and Dance

City Center of Music and Dance ⓬

Map 5B. West 55th St.

This highly ornate Moorish structure, with its dome of Spanish tiles, was designed in 1924 as a Shriners' Temple, then in 1943 home to the New York City Opera and Ballet. After the companies moved out, it became a major venue for touring dance companies.

Carnegie Hall ⓭

Map 5B. West 57th St. Museum open Thu–Tue and after concerts. Free.

The world's greatest visiting musicians play in this historic terra-cotta and brick

Auditorium of the Shubert Theater, built by Henry Herts in 1913

Renaissance concert hall (1891), with its superb acoustics. In 1964 it was made a national landmark. A 1986 renovation revitalized the ornamental plaster and bronze balconies. Musical memorabilia fill the corridors and museum.

Intrepid *Museum is on a large aircraft carrier on the Hudson River*

Intrepid Sea-Air-Space Museum ⓮

Map 6B. Pier 86, West 46th St. Open daily Apr–Sep, Tue–Sun Oct–Mar including public hols. Adm charge.

On the WWII US aircraft carrier *Intrepid*, exhibits include 1940s fighter planes, the world's fastest spy plane (A-12), and the guided-missile *Growler* submarine. You can board the famous *Concorde*, or see supercarriers in Stern Hall and flight simulators and rockets in Technologies Hall. Mission Control offers live coverage of NASA shuttles.

STREET LIFE

RESTAURANTS

Becco
Map 5B. 355 West 46th St.
Tel (212) 397 7597.
Moderate
Antipasti, salads, pastas, main courses, pre-theater menus.

Orso
Map 5B. 322 West 46th St.
Tel (212) 489 7212.
Moderate
Cheerful décor, open kitchen, pizza, pasta, Italian wine list.

Virgil's Real Barbecue
Map 5C. 152 West 44th St.
Tel (212) 921 9494.
Moderate
Ten different meat platters.

BARS AND CAFÉS

BP Café
Map 5C. Bryant Park.
A bar with a view. Popular midtown scene.

Broadway Diner
Map 5C. 1726 Broadway.
Thick-cut chips, corned beef hash with poached eggs.

Café Edison
Map 5B. Edison Hotel,
228 West 47th St.
Reasonably priced food in an Art Nouveau setting.

Chez Josephine
Map 5C. 414 West 42nd St.
Exuberant bistro-cabaret, live jazz piano, French food.

Lobby
Map 5A. Hudson Hotel,
356 West 58th St.
Glass-floored bar in trendy hotel. A regular hotspot.

P. J. Carney's
Map 5B. 906 7th Ave.
Irish ales, shepherd's pie.
See p96 for price codes.

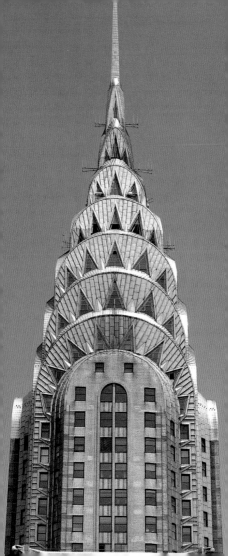

LOWER MIDTOWN

From Beaux Arts to Art Deco, Lower Midtown boasts some of the city's finest architecture. By 1900, many of New York's first families, including J.P. Morgan, lived here, their homes showing the grandeur of the age. Today's commercial pace quickens at 42nd Street, where tall office buildings line the streets near Grand Central.

SIGHTS AT A GLANCE

Historic Streets and Buildings
Grand Central Terminal **2**
Home Savings of America **3**
Chrysler Building **4**
Daily News Building **5**
Tudor City **6**
Fred F. French Building **9**

Museums and Galleries
Japan Society **8**
Morgan Library **11**

Modern Architecture
MetLife Building **1**
United Nations **7**

Churches
Church of the Incarnation **10**

SEE ALSO

• *Street Life p57*

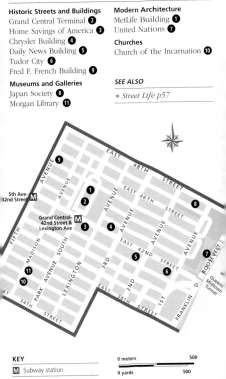

KEY

M Subway station	

0 meters	500
0 yards	500

◀ *The stainless-steel-coated spire of the Chrysler Building*

MetLife Building ❶

Map 4B. Park Ave. Open office hours. Free

Once, the sculptures atop Grand Central Terminal stood out against the skyline. Then this colossus, owned by Pan Am, rose up in 1963 to block the Park Avenue view. It dwarfed the terminal and aroused universal dislike. At the time it was the world's largest commercial building. In 1981 it was sold to Metropolitan Life.

Grand Central Terminal ❷

Map 4C. East 42nd St between Park and Lexington Aves. Open daily. Free guided tours Wed, Fri.

One of the world's great rail terminals, this outstanding Beaux Arts 1913 building is resplendent after its recent restoration. The soaring main concourse is suffused with natural light streaming in from windows all around and twinkling stars decorate the cerulean blue, vaulted

ceiling. Restaurants, shops, a gourmet food market, an oyster bar, and a museum attract 500,000 visitors daily.

Carved detail in the banking hall of Home Savings of America

Home Savings of America ❸

Map 4C. East 42nd St. Open by appt only. Free.

This 1923 Romanesque basilica-style building has an arched entry leading into a vast banking room, with a high beamed ceiling, mosaic floors, and marble columns supporting stone arches. Between the columns are mosaic panels; the rich detail has symbolic animal motifs (a squirrel for thrift).

Grand Central Terminal's vast main concourse with its high vaulted ceiling is dominated by three great arched windows on either side

Chrysler Building ❹

Map 4C. 405 Lexington Ave.
Open office hours (lobby only).

The shimmering spire of this 77-story, 1,046-ft-tall (320-m) building is one of New York's most-loved landmarks. Symbolizing the golden age of motoring, the stainless-steel Art Deco spire resembles a car radiator grill. The building's stepped setbacks are emblazoned with winged radiator caps, wheels, and stylized automobiles; there are stainless-steel gargoyles modeled on hood ornaments. The stunning lobby, lavishly decorated with marble, granite, and chromed steel trim, and its vast painted ceiling, was perfectly restored in 1978.

Daily News Building ❺

Map 3C. 220 East 42nd St.
Open Mon–Fri. Free.

This 1930 Art Deco classic has rows of brown and black brick alternating with windows to create a vertical striped effect. The lobby has the world's largest interior globe, and bronze lines on the floor indicate the direction of world cities and the position of the planets. At night, the intricate detail over its front entrance is lit from within by neon.

Stainless-steel gargoyle on the Chrysler Building

Tudor City ❻

Map 3C. East 41st–43rd St, between 1st and 2nd Aves. Free.

This 1928 urban renewal effort, designed as a middle-class city within the city, has 12 buildings containing 3,000 apartments, a hotel, shops, restaurants, a post office, and two small private parks, all built in the American Tudor Gothic style. The complex has only a few windows that have views of the once shabby East River shore.

Upper stories of Tudor City

Delegates at the horseshoe-shaped table in the Security Council at the United Nations

United Nations **7**

Map 3C. 1st Ave at 46th St. Open daily Mar–Dec, Mon–Fri Jan–Feb except public hols. Adm charge for tours.

Founded in 1945, the UN now numbers 189 nations. Its goals are to preserve global peace, aid social and economic well-being in the world, and promote self-determination. It is made up of the Secretariat, the General Assembly, and three Councils: Security; Economic and Social; and Trusteeship. The 18-acre (7-ha) site is an international zone; it has its own stamps and post office.

Japan Society **8**

Map 3B. East 47th St. Gallery open Tue–Sun. Free.

This striking black 1971 building, with its delicate sun grilles, houses an auditorium, language center, research library, museum gallery, and traditional Oriental gardens. Various Japanese arts, from swords to kimonos and scrolls, are on show, plus programs of Japanese performing arts, lectures, language classes, and business workshops.

Fred F. French Building **9**

Map 4B. 5th Ave. Open office hours. Free.

This fabulously opulent 1927 creation is a handsome blend of Near Eastern, ancient Egyptian and Greek, and early Art Deco styles. Multicolored faïence ornaments decorate the upper façade, while winged Assyrian beasts ride on a bronze frieze over the entrance. The vaulted lobby has an elaborate polychrome ceiling decoration and 25 gilt-bronze doors.

Magnificent vaulted lobby in the Fred F. French Building

Church of the Incarnation **10**

Map 4C. Madison Ave. Open daily. Guided tours by appt. Free.

The patterned sandstone and brownstone exterior of this 1864 episcopal church is typical of the period. The splendid interior includes an oak communion rail by

Daniel Chester French; a chancel mural, *Adoration of the Magi*, by John La Farge; and stained-glass windows by La Farge, Louis Comfort Tiffany, William Morris, and Edward Burne-Jones.

Morgan Library ⓫

Map 4C. East 36th St. Open Tue–Sun except public hols. Adm charge.

This magnificent *palazzo*-style building was designed, in 1902, to house the collection of billionaire J. Pierpont Morgan, an extraordinary

Exquisite 1455 Gutenberg Bible, printed on vellum, Morgan Library

assemblage of rare manuscripts, books, and prints. Highlights include the exquisite West and East Rooms and the elegant Rotunda. The library is being expanded and will reopen in 2006.

STREET LIFE

RESTAURANTS

Asia de Cuba
Map 4C. 237 Madison Ave. Tel (212) 726 7755.
Expensive
Minimalist-chic white dining room. Latin fusion with Asian touches.

Grand Central Oyster Bar and Restaurant
Map 4C. Grand Central Terminal, lower level. Tel (212) 490 6650.
Moderate
Bustling and ever-popular New York classic, serving the freshest seafood. A lengthy Californian wine list.

Michael Jordan's The Steakhouse NYC
Map 4C. Grand Central Terminal, north balcony. Tel (212) 655 2300.
Expensive
Expect high-quality, dry, aged cuts. You can't beat the view of the train passengers below.

See p96 for price codes.

BARS

Beer Bar
Map 4C. Café Centro, 200 Park Ave.
Art Deco-style singles bar. Interesting beer list and beer-tasting menus.

The Cigar Room at Trumpets
Map 4C. Grand Hyatt Hotel, Grand Central Terminal, East 42nd Street.
Glass-enclosed space above the lobby in the Grand Hyatt Hotel. Separated private enclaves. Very pleasant on winter afternoons when the sun streams through the glass.

SHOPPING

Department Stores
Map 4B. 5th Ave, between 38th and 58 Sts.
Bountiful stocks of beautiful clothing await at such elegant shops as Bergdorf Goodman, Saks Fifth Avenue, Lord & Taylor, and Bloomingdales.

AVENUE OF THE AME

W 54

7

5 8

W 52ND

UPPER MIDTOWN

Upscale New York in all its diversity is here, with museums, churches, synagogues, grand hotels, famous stores, and trend-setting skyscrapers. From 1833, the area was home to high society, but in the 1950s, modern office buildings marked its change from residential to business.

SIGHTS AT A GLANCE

Historic Streets and Buildings
Villard Houses **10**
Roosevelt Island **15**
Fuller Building **16**

Modern Architecture
Trump Tower **2**
IBM Building **3**
Seagram Building **12**
Citigroup Center **13**

Museums and Galleries
Museum of Arts and Design **5**
Museum of Modern Art (MoMA) **6**

American Folk Art Museum **7**
Museum of Television and Radio **8**

Churches and Synagogues
St. Thomas Church **4**
St. Patrick's Cathedral pp62–3 **9**
Central Synagogue **14**

Landmark Hotels
Waldorf–Astoria **11**

Landmark Stores
Fifth Avenue **1**

SEE ALSO

• Street Life p65

◀ The Museum of Modern Art on 54th Street

Window display at Bergdorf
Goodman on Fifth Avenue at 57th

Fifth Avenue ❶

Map 4B.

Fifth Avenue is New York's
best-known boulevard and
a mecca for luxury goods,
such as Cartier, Bergdorf
Goodman, Bloomingdales,
Saks Fifth Avenue, Tiffany,
and Lord & Taylor. After
William Henry Vanderbilt
erected his mansion at Fifth
Avenue and 51st Street in
1883, palatial homes were
built as far as Central Park.

Trump Tower ❷

Map 4B. Fifth Avenue. Open
daily. Free.

A glittering, expensive 1983
apartment and office tower
rises above a lavish six-story
atrium with layers of
exclusive shops and cafés.
This opulent example of the
trend toward vertical shopping centers boasts hanging
gardens and a spectacular
80-ft (24-m) waterfall. Next
door is a complete contrast:
Tiffany & Co., the prestigious jewelers founded in
1837 and immortalized by
Truman Capote in his 1958
novel *Breakfast at Tiffany's*.

IBM Building ❸

Map 4B. Madison Ave. Garden
Plaza open daily. Museum open
Tue—Sun except public hols.
Adm free 6–9pm.

This 43-story 1983 tower is
a sleek, five-sided prism of
gray-green polished granite,
with a cantilevered corner
at 57th Street. The Garden
Plaza is open to the public;
and the Dahesh Museum
has European paintings,
drawings, and sculptures.

St. Thomas Church ❹

Map 4B. West 53rd St.
Open daily. Free.

This 1914 limestone building, in French-Gothic style,
has a single asymmetrical
tower and an off-center
nave. Inside are richly
carved, shimmering white
screens behind the altar and
carvings (from the 1920s) in
the choir stalls of modern
inventions and Presidents
Roosevelt and Wilson.

Interior carvings by sculptor Lee
Lawrie in St. Thomas Church

Museum of Arts and Design ⑤

Map 5B. West 53rd St.
Open daily except public hols.
Adm charge.

The leading American cultural institution of its kind, this museum exhibits an array of contemporary objects, ranging from clay and glass to wood, metal, and fiber. The permanent collection, dating from 1900, includes over 2,000 artifacts by international craftsmen and designers. It will move to Columbus Circle in 2007.

Beautiful, restful sculpture garden at the Museum of Modern Art

Museum of Modern Art (MoMA) ⑥

Map 4B. West 53rd St, between Fifth Ave & Ave of the Americas.
Open Wed–Mon except Dec 25.
Adm charge.

MoMA contains one of the world's most comprehensive collections of modern art. Its 150,000 works range from artists such as Van Gogh and Picasso to Lichtenstein, Warhol, and early masterpieces of photography and film, too. Founded in 1929, it set the standard for museums of its kind. After an expansion program, it reopened in 2004, almost doubling its display space.

American Folk Art Museum ⑦

Map 5B. West 53rd St.
Open Tue–Sun. Free.

The permanent home for the appreciation and study of American folk art is in the first free-standing art museum built in New York since 1966. Clad in panels of white tombasil, it has 30,000 sq ft (2,787 sq m) of exhibition space on eight levels.

Museum of Television and Radio ⑧

Map 4B. West 52nd St.
Open Tue–Sun except public hols.
Adm charge.

In this one-of-a-kind museum (a hi-tech building that looks like an antique radio set), watch and listen to news, entertainment, and sports from television and radio's earliest days to the present, from a catalog of over 50,000 programs. There are retrospectives of artists and directors, posters, photo exhibits, and memorabilia.

The hi-tech, one-of-a-kind Museum of Television and Radio looks like an antique radio set

St. Patrick's Cathedral ⑨

See pp62–3.

St. Patrick's Cathedral ❾

In 1878, New York's finest Gothic Revival building, the US's largest Catholic cathedral, was erected. The bronze doors, baldachin over the high altar, Lady Chapel, great organ, and rose window are among its notable features. Side altars are dedicated to saints and holy figures.

The Pièta, *created in 1906, stands at the side of the Lady Chapel.*

The Great Baldachin *over the high altar is made of bronze. Statues of saints and prophets adorn the four piers.*

The Shrine of St. Elizabeth Ann Seton

VISITORS' CHECKLIST

Map 4B. 5th Avenue and 50th Street. Tel (212) 753 2261. Open daily. Church services frequent Mon–Sat, Sun. Shop. Wheelchair access. Concerts & lectures.

The Lady Chapel *honors the Blessed Virgin, and the stained-glass windows portray the mysteries of the rosary.*

The Stations of the Cross Reliefs *were carved of Caen stone in Holland.*

The 26-ft (8-m) Rose Window *shines above the great organ, which has more than 7,000 pipes.*

The Bronze Doors *weigh 20,000 lb (9,000 kg).*

Main entrance

The Cathedral's Façade *is built of white marble, the two spires rising 330 ft (101 m) above.*

Villard Houses ⑩

Map 4B. Madison Ave (New York Palace Hotel). Urban Center open Mon–Sat. Free.

In 1881, publisher Henry Villard built six four-story houses, set round a central court opening to the street. In the 1970s, the air rights were bought for the 51-story Helmsley (now New York) Palace Hotel. The center wing is the hotel's entrance. The Urban Center, in the north wing, has a great bookshop on architecture.

Waldorf–Astoria ⑪

Map 4B. Park Ave.

This 1931 Art Deco classic covers an entire city block. Still one of New York's most prestigious hotels, it is a reminder of a more glamorous era. The 625-ft (190-m) twin towers have hosted many celebrities, including presidents and royalty. Of note are Cole Porter's piano in the cocktail lounge and the giant lobby clock.

The Art Deco Waldorf–Astoria

The pool at the Four Seasons in the Seagram Building

Seagram Building ⑫

Map 4B. Park Ave.
Open Mon–Fri. Free.

The only New York building by Mies van der Rohe is a Modernist 1950s "glass box" with slender bands of bronze amid walls of smoked glass rising from the horizontal open plaza. Within is Philip Johnson's glass-walled lobby blurring the division between indoor and outdoor space, and the Four Seasons Restaurant.

Citigroup Center ⑬

Map 4B. East 53rd St. Open daily. Church open daily, jazz vespers Sun, concerts noon Wed.

An aluminum-clad spire built on ten-story stilts with a sliced-off roof, the 1978 Citigroup Center is unique, an unmistakable landmark on the city skyline. It incorporates St. Peter's Lutheran Church, a granite sculpture below a corner of the tower, and inside is the striking Erol Beker Chapel.

Central Synagogue ⑭

Map 4B. Lexington Ave. Open Tue–Wed. Services Fri–Sat. Free.

This is New York's oldest building in continuous use as a synagogue. Restored after a 1999 fire, this 1870 design is the city's best example of Moorish-Islamic Revival architecture. Its brownstone façade has twin towers topped by 122-ft (37-m) domed minarets. The stenciled interior is a mix of red, blue, ocher, and gilt.

Elie Nadelman's clock statues above Fuller Building entrance

Roosevelt Island 15

Map 3B.

A Swiss cable car across the East River or a tram departing from 2nd Avenue at 60th Street offer thrilling rides and fine views of the city. The 147-acre (59-ha) island, once called "Welfare Island," was redeveloped in the 1970s, to create a quiet, traffic-free residential community of 3,000 apartments.

Fuller Building 16

Map 4A. East 57th St.
Open Tue–Sat. Free.

This slim-towered, black, gray, and white 1929 beauty is a prime example of geometric Art Deco design. Above the entrance are striking statues on either side of the clock. Inside are intricate mosaic tile floors and exclusive art galleries, most open daily.

STREET LIFE

RESTAURANTS

La Bonne Soupe
Map 4B. 48 West 55th St, between 5th & 6th Aves.
Tel (212) 586 7650. **Moderate**
Old-fashioned French bistro.

Brasserie
Map 4B. 100 East 53rd St at Lexington Ave.
Tel (212) 751 4940.
Moderate
French-American dishes.

Le Cirque 2000
Map 4B. Palace Hotel, 455 Madison Ave at 50th St.
Tel (212) 303 7788. **Moderate**
Award-winning cuisine.

Four Seasons
Map 4B. 99 East 52nd St at Park Ave.
Tel (212) 754 9494. **Moderate**
A New York institution.

SHOPPING

Designer Boutiques
Map 4A. 57th St, between 5th & Madison Aves.
Burberry, Hermès, Chanel, Dior, and Prada.

H&M
Map 4B. 5th Ave at 51st St.
Great young fashion with small price tags.

Niketown
Map 4A. 6 East 57th St, between 5th & Madison Avs.
Hi-tech shopping fun. Great sportswear.

Takashimaya
Map 4B. 5th Ave, between 54th & 55th Sts.
New York home of a leading Japanese department store.

See p96 for price codes.

UPPER EAST SIDE

Around 1900, New York society moved to this area. Today, their Beaux Arts mansions, now embassies and museums, are clustered along Fifth Avenue's Museum Mile. The city's elite still occupy grand apartment buildings, but farther east are German and Czech shops and churches.

SIGHTS AT A GLANCE

Historic Buildings
Seventh Regiment Armory ⑩

Museums and Galleries
Neue Galerie New York ①
Jewish Museum ②
Cooper-Hewitt National Design Museum ③
National Academy Museum ④
Solomon R. Guggenheim Museum ⑤
Metropolitan Museum of Art ⑥
Whitney Museum of American Art ⑦
Frick Collection ⑧
Asia Society ⑨
Society of Illustrators ⑪
Mount Vernon Hotel Museum and Garden ⑫
Museum of the City of New York ⑮

Churches
Church of the Holy Trinity ⑬
St. Nicholas Russian Orthodox Cathedral ⑭

SEE ALSO

• *Street Life p71*

KEY

Ⓜ Subway station

0 meters   500
0 yards   500

◀ *One of a few wooden houses left in Manhattan, on East 92nd Street*

Neue Galerie New York ❶

Map 2O. 5th Avenue at East 86th St. Open Fri–Mon except public hols. Adm charge.

This Louis XIII-style, Beaux Arts mansion of 1914, one of Fifth Avenue's most distinguished, is designated a landmark. The museum has a fine collection of German and Austrian decorative arts of the early 1900s. Exhibits include works by Klimt, Kandinsky, Schiele, Klee, and the Bauhaus. The Café Sabarsky draws inspiration from Viennese cafés of old.

The decorative arts are well represented at the Cooper-Hewitt National Design Museum

Jewish Museum ❷

Map 2O. 5th Avenue. Open Sun–Fri except Sat, public, Jewish hols. Adm charge.

The exquisite, château-like museum of 1908 houses one of the world's largest collections of Jewish art. Covering 4,000 years, artifacts include Torah crowns, a Torah ark, candelabras, plates, kiddush cups, scrolls, silver ceremonial objects, and the exquisite faience entrance wall of a 16th-century Persian synagogue.

Cooper-Hewitt National Design Museum ❸

Map 2O. East 91st St. Open Tue–Sun except public hols. Adm charge.

One of the world's largest design collections is in the former home of industrialist Andrew Carnegie. The museum opened in 1897 at Cooper Union, but in 1967 the Smithsonian Institution acquired the collections, and the Carnegie Corporation offered the mansion. Visitors can still enjoy the fine wooden staircase, rich paneling and carving, and a sunny solarium.

National Academy Museum ❹

Map 2O. 5th Ave. Open Wed–Sun except public hols. Adm charge.

More than 6,000 paintings, drawings, and sculptures, including works by Winslow Homer, Raphael Soyer, and Frank Lloyd Wright, comprise the museum's collection, founded in 1825 by a group of artists. The attractive building boasts patterned marble floors, decorative plaster ceilings, and a grand entrance foyer.

Statue of Diana in National Academy Museum's foyer

Solomon R. Guggenheim Museum ❺

Map 2O. 5th Avenue at 88th St. Open Fri–Wed except Dec 25, Jan 1. Adm charge.

Home to one of the finest modern and contemporary art collections in the world, the building itself is a masterpiece. Designed by Frank Lloyd Wright, the shell-like façade is a New York landmark. Its spiral ramp curves down from the dome, passing works by major 19th-, 20th-, and 21st-century artists. It remains open while the building's exterior is being restored.

Floodlit at dusk, the Guggenheim Museum looks purple

Metropolitan Museum of Art ❻

Map 2P. 5th Avenue. Open Tue–Sun except public hols. Adm charge.

One of the world's great art museums, its collection spans 5,000 years of culture from all the continents. The Gothic Revival building of 1880 has over two million holdings, dating from prehistoric times to the present. It was founded by a group

of artists who dreamed of an American art institution to rival those of Europe. An Etruscan gallery and a Roman Court open in 2007.

Elegant entrance to the Metropolitan Museum of Art

Whitney Museum of American Art ❼

Map 2P. Madison Ave. Open Wed–Sun except public hols. Adm charge.

The museum, founded in 1930 by sculptor Gertrude Vanderbilt Whitney, is the foremost showcase for American 20th- and 21st-century art. In 1966 it moved to this inverted-pyramid building. The Whitney Biennial, the most significant survey of new trends in US art, is held in even years.

Frick Collection ❽

Map 2P. East 70th St. Open Tue–Sun except most public hols. Adm charge.

The priceless art collection of steel magnate Henry Clay Frick is exhibited in this residential setting amid the furnishings of his opulent mansion. On his death, he bequeathed the entire house to the nation. The collection includes important Old Master paintings, Oriental rugs, rare Limoges enamels, and fine French furniture.

Asia Society **9**

Map 2P. Park Ave. Open Tue–Sun except public hols. Adm charge.

Founded in 1956 by John D. Rockefeller III to aid understanding of Asian culture, this eight-story, red granite 1981 building is a forum for 30 countries ranging from Japan to Iran, Central Asia to Australia. After renovation in 2001, its space has greatly increased, offering Asian arts, films, dance, concerts, lectures, and a well-stocked bookshop.

Entrance hall, 7th Regiment Armory

Seventh Regiment Armory **10**

Map 4A. Park Ave. Open by appt Mon–Fri except public hols. Free.

The socially prominent members of this regiment of 1805 built a remarkable armory in 1877–89. Its drill room stands 200 by 300 ft (60 by 90 m) and 100 ft (30 m) high, while the administration building resembles a medieval fortress, its lavish rooms filled with lavish Victorian furnishings, objets d'art, and regimental memorabilia.

Society of Illustrators **11**

Map 4A. East 63rd St. Open Tue–Sat except public hols. Free.

The notable roster of this society, formed in 1901 to promote the illustrator's art, included Charles Dana Gibson, N.C. Wyeth, and Howard Pyle. The Museum of American Illustration opened in 1981, to show the history of magazine and book illustration, with an annual exhibition of the finest American illustrations.

Mount Vernon Hotel Museum and Garden **12**

Map 3A. East 61st St. Open Tue–Sun except Aug, public hols. Adm charge.

The 1799 Mount Vernon Hotel Museum and Garden, once a country day hotel, was recreated as a charming Federal home in 1924. Costumed guides show the treasure-filled rooms full of Chinese porcelain, Sheraton chests, Aubusson carpets, and a Duncan Phyfe sofa.

Church of the Holy Trinity **13**

Map 1O. East 88th St. Open Sun–Fri. Services Tue, Sun. Free.

Delightfully placed in a serene garden setting, this French Renaissance-style church (1889) was built of glowing golden brick and terra-cotta. It boasts one of New York's best bell towers, which holds a handsome wrought-iron clock with brass hands. The arched doorway is richly decorated with carved images of the saints and prophets.

Ornate St. Nicholas Cathedral

Museum of the City of New York 15

Map 2N. 5th Ave at 103rd St. Open Tue–Sun except public hols.

Housed in a handsome Georgian Colonial building, the museum (founded 1923) illustrates New York's history, with period rooms, costumes, photographs, paintings, silver, a large collection of Currier & Ives hand-colored lithographs, toys, dolls, dollhouses, and other memorabilia.

St. Nicholas Russian Orthodox Cathedral 14

Map 2N. East 97th St. Open by appt. Services in Russian. Free.

This Baroque-style cathedral (1902) has five onion domes and blue and yellow tiles on a red brick and white stone façade. Inside are marble columns, trimmed blue and white, and golden screens.

Elegant façade, City of NY Museum

STREET LIFE

RESTAURANTS

davidburke & donatella
Map 4A. 133 East 61st St, between Lexington & Park Aves. Tel (212) 813 2121.
Moderate
New American cuisine.

Orsay
Map 2P. 1057–1059 Lexington Ave at 75th St.
Tel (212) 517 6400.
Moderate
Chic French café, bistro fare.

Payard Bistro
Map 2P. 1032 Lexington Ave at 77th St. Tel (212) 717 5252.
Moderate
Superb French food.

SHOPPING

BCBG Max Azria
Map 4A. 770 Madison Ave at 66th St.
Hot designer, sexy fashion.

Bottega Veneta
Map 4A. 635 Madison Ave, between 59th & 60th Sts.
Luxury leather goods, shoes.

Shanghai Tang
Map 4A. 714 Madison Ave, between 63rd & 64th Sts.
Fashion, home furnishings.

See p96 for price codes.

CENTRAL PARK

The city's "backyard" was transformed in 1858 from quarries, swampland, pig farms, and shacks into today's lush 843-acre (340-ha) park. Scenic hills, lakes, meadows, trees, and shrubs make a superb setting for its playgrounds, ball fields, tennis courts, skating rinks, and concerts. Cars are banned on weekends, giving bicyclists, joggers, and rollerbladers the right-of-way.

SIGHTS AT A GLANCE

Historic Buildings
The Dairy ❶
Belvedere Castle ❸

Monuments and Statues
Strawberry Fields ❷
Bow Bridge ❹
Bethesda Fountain and
  Terrace ❺

Lakes and Gardens
Conservatory Water ❻
Central Park Wildlife
  Center ❼
Conservatory
  Garden ❽

KEY

Ⓜ Subway station

◀ Bird's-eye view of Central Park

A Tour of Central Park

A walking tour from 59th to 79th Streets takes in some of the park's loveliest features, from the wooded Ramble to the formal Bethesda Terrace. Artificial lakes, graceful arches, and bridges link 58 miles (93 km) of footpaths and roads. In summer the park is a cool retreat away from hot streets.

Strawberry Fields
is a much-visited area of peace in memory of John Lennon. ❷

Wollman Rink
was restored in the 1980s for future generations of skaters.

The Dairy
houses the Visitor Center. ❶

CENTRAL PARK

SHEEP MEADOW

THE MALL

CENTRAL PARK SOUTH

FIFTH

Plaza Hotel

The Pond

Frick Collection
(see p69)

Central Park Wildlife Center has three climate zones, home to over 100 animal species. ❼

Hans Christian Andersen's statue is a favorite landmark for children.

The Cast-iron Bow Bridge *links Cherry Hill and the Ramble by a graceful arch, 60 ft (18 m) above the Lake.* ❹

Dakota Building, *where Yoko Ono and John Lennon lived.*

Bethesda Fountain *and the richly ornamented formal terrace overlook the Lake and the wooded shores of the Ramble.* ❺

San Remo Apartments (see p80)

American Museum of Natural History *(see p81)*

GREAT LAWN

Metropolitan Museum of Art *(see p69)*

Obelisk

Guggenheim Museum *(see p69)*

Conservatory Water *is the scene of model boat races each Saturday from Mar–Nov.* ❻

Alice in Wonderland *is immortalized in bronze at the northern end of Conservatory Water, along with the Cheshire Cat, the Mad Hatter and the Dormouse.*

Belvedere Castle *houses the Central Park Learning Center. Its terraces give unequaled views of the city and surrounding park.* ❸

The Dairy ❶

Map 5A. Open Tue–Sun. Free.

This charming Victorian Gothic stone building was planned as part of the "Children's District," to include a Children's Cottage, playground, stable, and the Carousel. Maps and park events are available from the Dairy, used as Central Park's Visitor Center. Here is the place to begin exploring the lush and leafy park.

Strawberry Fields ❷

Map 3P.

The restoration of this teardrop-shaped section of the park was Yoko Ono's tribute to her slain husband, John Lennon. Gifts for the garden came from all over the world. A mosaic set in the pathway, inscribed with *Imagine* (for Lennon's famous song), was a gift from Naples in Italy.

Belvedere Castle with its lookout over the park

Belvedere Castle ❸

Map 3P. Open Tue–Sun. Free.

This stone castle atop Vista Rock, complete with tower and turrets, offers one of the best views of the park and the city from its rooftop lookout. Inside is the Henry Luce Nature Observatory, with a delightful exhibit telling inquisitive young visitors about the park's surprising variety of wildlife.

Bow Bridge ❹

Map 3P.

One of the park's seven original cast-iron bridges, Bow Bridge is considered one of the finest and was designed as a bow tying together the two large sections of the Lake. In the 1800s, when the Lake was used for ice skating, a red ball would be hoisted from a bell tower on Vista Rock to signal the ice was safe for skating.

Exclusive apartments overlooking Central Park

Bethesda Fountain and Terrace ❺

Map 3P.

Bethesda Fountain, a tranquil oasis in Central Park

Bethesda Fountain, named after the pool of Bethesda in Jerusalem, was dedicated in 1873. Situated between the Lake and the Mall, this is Central Park's architectural heart, a formal element in the naturalistic landscape. The statue, *Angel of the Waters*, marked the opening of the Croton Aqueduct system in 1842, bringing the city its first supply of pure water. The Spanish-style detailing has tiles, friezes, and a sculptured double staircase.

Conservatory Water ❻

Map 2P.

This stretch of water is home to model boat races every weekend. At the lake's north end, children delight in the sculpture of Alice in Wonderland. On the west bank, free story hours are held at a statue of Hans Christian Andersen. Like that of Alice, small children love climbing on this statue, to snuggle in the author's lap.

Central Park Wildlife Center ❼

Map 4A. Open daily. Adm charge.

Praised for its creative use of small space, this imaginative zoo has more than 130 species of animals from three climate zones: Polar Circle, California coast, and Tropics. Penguins and polar bears populate an Arctic landscape while a rain forest has monkeys and free-flying birds. The Tisch Children's Zoo has goats, sheep, cows, and pot-bellied pigs. The whimsical, much-loved Delacorte Clock plays nursery rhymes as its bronze musical animals go round.

Polar bear in the Central Park Wildlife Center

Conservatory Garden ❽

Map 2N. Open daily. Free.

This 6-acre (2.4-ha) park contains three formal gardens, each of a different landscape style. The Italian Central Garden has a large lawn, yew hedges, crabapple trees, and a wisteria pergola. The English South Garden spills over with perennials, with a bronze statue in the reflecting pool. The French North Garden centers around the bronze, *Fountain of the Three Dancing Maidens.*

UPPER WEST SIDE

This area became residential in the 1870s, when the Ninth Avenue elevated railroad made commuting to midtown possible. In 1884, the first apartment house was built, followed by buildings on Central Park West and Broadway. Cross streets still have fine brownstone row houses. Now it's filled with diverse cultural institutions.

SIGHTS AT A GLANCE

Historic Buildings
Twin Towers of Central
Park West ❶

Museums and Galleries
New-York Historical
Society ❻
American Museum of Natural
History ❼
Hayden Planetarium ❽
Children's Museum of
Manhattan ❾

Famous Theaters
Lincoln Center for the
Performing Arts ❷
New York State
Theater ❸

Metropolitan Opera
House ❹
Lincoln Center Theater ❺

SEE ALSO

● *Street Life p81*

0 meters 500
0 yards 500

KEY

Ⓜ Subway station

◀ *The façade of 14 Riverside Drive*

The famous Twin Towers, or San Remo Apartments, of Central Park West, designed by Emery Roth

Twin Towers of Central Park West ❶

Map 5A. Closed to the public.

The four twin-towered apartment houses on Central Park West (at 25, 115, 145, and 300) are familiar landmarks on the city skyline. They are admired today for their grace and architectural detail, such as setbacks and towers. Famous tenants included Marilyn Monroe and Groucho Marx.

Lincoln Center for the Performing Arts ❷

Map 6A.

In 1959, the city's most important cultural center was born, covering 15 acres (6 ha) of a slum site. Today, it houses an array of venues for opera, classical music, and ballet. In summer, the popular Mostly Mozart and free concerts take place.

New York State Theater ❸

Map 6A. Lincoln Center.

This 2,800-seat theater, home of the highly acclaimed New York City Ballet and Opera companies, was built in 1964. The vast four-story foyer is dominated by huge white marble sculptures. It is called "a little jewel box," because of chandeliers and rhinestone lights both inside and out.

Metropolitan Opera House ❹

Map 6A. Lincoln Center.

Home to the Metropolitan Opera Company and the American Ballet Theater, "the Met" is the most spectacular of Lincoln Center's buildings. Five great arched windows offer views of the opulent foyer and two radiant murals by Marc Chagall. Inside are curved white marble stairs, plush red carpeting, and exquisite starburst crystal chandeliers.

Central plaza at Lincoln Center

Lincoln Center Theater ❺

Map 6A. Lincoln Center.

Two theaters (the 1,000-seat Vivian Beaumont and the 280-seat Mitzi E. Newhouse) make up this innovative complex, presenting eclectic and often experimental drama. Nearby is the New York Public Library for the Performing Arts, with audio cylinders of early Met performances, playbills, and original scores on show.

New-York Historical Society ❻

Map 3P. Central Park West. Galleries open Tue–Sat. Adm charge. Library Tue–Sun (Tue–Fri in summer). Closed public hols.

This 1804 society, the city's oldest museum and research library, houses historical material on 18th-century newspapers, slavery and the Civil War, Tiffany lamps and glasswork, American furniture and silver, and all 435 watercolors of Audubon's *Birds of America*.

Four mounted African elephants at Museum of Natural History

American Museum of Natural History ❼

Map 3P. Central Park West at 79th St. Open daily. Donations.

One of the world's largest natural history museums, the complex now covers four city blocks. It has over 30 million specimens and artifacts. Most popular are the dinosaurs, and the Milstein Hall of Ocean Life. The new Rose Center for Earth and Space includes the Hayden Planetarium.

Hayden Planetarium ❽

Map 3P. Central Park West at 81st St.

The spectacular centerpiece of the Rose Center, it stands within a three-story, 87-ft (26-m) sphere inside a huge glass cube. Features include a technologically advanced Space Theater, the 350-ft (107-m) Cosmic Pathway, and a Big Bang Theater.

Children's Museum of Manhattan ❾

Map 4O. West 83rd St. Open Wed–Sun (Jul & Aug, Tue–Sun), except public hols. Adm charge.

Features of this imaginative, hands-on museum include a Body Odyssey, Centers for inventions and media, storytellers, puppeteers, making books, and Word Play area.

STREET LIFE

RESTAURANTS

Fiorello's Café
Map 5A. 1900 Broadway, between 63rd & 64th Sts.
Tel (212) 595 5330.
Moderate
Bountiful antipasto bar.

Picholine
Map 5A. 36 West 64th St at Broadway. Tel (212) 724 8585.
Moderate
Elegant Mediterranean dining.

BARS

Journeys
Map 5A. Essex House Hotel, 160 Central Park South.
This hotel bar has an English club ambience.

Tavern on the Green
Map 5A. Central Park West at 67th St.
Glitzy inside, with magical views of Central Park.

See p96 for price codes.

MORNINGSIDE HEIGHTS AND HARLEM

Morningside Heights is home to Columbia University and a fine cathedral. Farther east is Hamilton Heights, on the border of Harlem, America's most famous black community. From here take in the district's highlights, enjoy a gospel choir in the St. Nicholas Historic District, and end with a southern-style brunch at Sylvia's.

SIGHTS AT A GLANCE

Historic Buildings and Monuments
Columbia University ❶
Low Library ❷
Grant's Tomb ❺

Museums and Galleries
Studio Museum in Harlem ❼
Museo del Barrio ❽

Famous Theaters
Apollo Theater ❻

Churches
Cathedral of St. John the Divine ❸
Riverside Church ❹

SEE ALSO

• Street Life p85

KEY

Ⓜ Subway station

◀ *Sunday morning gospel service at Abyssinian Baptist Church, Harlem*

Columbia University's main courtyard graced by the classical Low Library

Columbia University ❶

Map 4M. Main entrance at West 116th St and Broadway.

Columbia, an Ivy League School and one of America's oldest universities, is noted for medicine, journalism, and law. It was founded in 1754 as King's College but moved in 1897 to its present campus of plazas and lawns on a serene terrace. Today, it has over 19,000 students.

Low Library ❷

Map 4M. Columbia University.

A classical, columned building atop three flights of stone stairs, the library is now used as offices and its rotunda for academic and ceremonial purposes. It was the site of anti-Vietnam War demonstrations in 1968.

Cathedral of St. John the Divine ❸

Map 4M. Amsterdam Ave at West 112th St. Open daily. Donations.

Over 600 ft (180 m) long and 146 ft (45 m) wide, this 1892 edifice is a mix of Romanesque and Gothic styles. Impressive features include the west entrance, the rose window, bay altars, and the Peace Fountain on the south lawn.

Riverside Church ❹

Map 4M. Riverside Dr at 122nd St. Open daily. Free.

A 21-story steel frame with a Gothic exterior, the design was inspired by Chartres Cathedral. The organ has 22,000 pipes, the carillon 74 bells. Its 21st-floor observation deck has fine views.

Grant's Tomb ❺

Map 4L. West 122nd St and Riverside Dr. Open daily except public hols. Free.

This grandiose 1897 mausoleum honors America's 18th president and contains coffins of him and his wife; each sarcophagus weighs 8.5 tons. Two rooms feature his life and career. On the north and east sides are 17 curved, mosaic benches.

Each gray granite column is 55 ft (17 m) tall in St. John the Divine

Apollo Theater **6**

Map 3L. West 125th St.
Open at showtimes. Groups only.

The Apollo began in 1913 as a whites-only opera house. When a white entrepreneur opened it to all races, the Apollo became Harlem's best-known showcase for artists like Ellington and Holiday. It still is a place to go for blues, jazz, and gospel.

The famous Apollo Theater

Studio Museum in Harlem **7**

Map 3L. West 125th St. Open Wed–Sun except public hols. Donations.

This five-story building (opened 1967) has a permanent collection of works by major black artists, a photographic archive of Harlem in its heyday, an artist-in-residence program, lectures, seminars, and film festivals.

Museo del Barrio **8**

Map 2N. 5th Ave. Open Wed–Sun except public hols. Adm charge.

North America's only museum for Latin American art (founded 1969) features folk art, contemporary painting and sculpture, and rare Pre-Columbian artifacts. Stars are the 240 carved wooden *Santos* statues.

STREET LIFE

RESTAURANTS

Bayou
Map 3L. 308 Lenox Ave at 125th St. Tel (212) 426 3800.
Moderate
Cajun is a specialty.

Jimmy's Uptown
Map 3L. 2207 Seventh Ave. Tel (212) 491 4000.
Cheap
Latin food for the soul.

Sylvia's
Map 3L. 328 Lenox Ave, between 126th & 127th Sts. Tel (212) 996 0660.
Cheap
Famous soul-food restaurant. Southern-fried chicken, spicy ribs. Gospel and brunch.

MUSIC VENUES

Aaron Davis Hall
Map 4K. City College campus, West 135th St & Convent Ave.
Home to jazz and opera.

Cotton Club
Map 3L. 656 West 125th St, near West 125th & Martin Luther King Jr. Blvd.
Famous 1920s club.

Showman's
Map 3L. 375 West 125th St, at St. Nicholas & Morningside Dr.
Live jazz, cool vibes.

See p96 for price codes.

FARTHER AFIELD

Though officially part of New York City, the boroughs outside Manhattan are quite different in feel and spirit. These outlying areas are residential, without any famous skyscrapers, and boast many attractions: the city's biggest zoo, botanical gardens, museums, beaches, and a wildlife center.

SIGHTS AT A GLANCE

Historic Streets and Buildings
George Washington
  Bridge **1**
Wave Hill **3**

Museums and Galleries
The Cloisters **2**
Brooklyn Children's
  Museum **6**
Brooklyn Museum **8**

Parks and Gardens
New York Botanical
  Garden **4**

Bronx Zoo/Wildlife
  Conservation Park **5**

Famous Theaters
Brooklyn Academy of Music
  (BAM) **7**

Beaches
Jamaica Bay Wildlife Refuge
  Center **9**

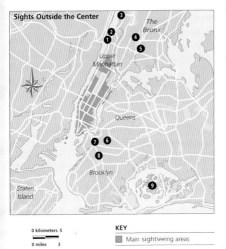

Sights Outside the Center

The Bronx

Upper Manhattan

Queens

Brooklyn

Staten Island

0 kilometers 5
0 miles 3

KEY

▨ Main sightseeing areas

◀ *Jamaica Bay*

George Washington Bridge ❶

175th St. Tolls.

This magnificent bridge, with a span of 3,500-ft (1,065-m), was completed in 1931; lack of funds left the two elegant, 600-ft (183-m) high skeletal towers unclad. A vital link for commuter traffic, tolls show 53 million eastbound cars each year. A lower deck was added in 1962. The lighthouse below the eastern tower was saved from demolition in 1951.

Vaulted ceiling of the Pontaut Chapter House in The Cloisters

The Cloisters ❷

Fort Tryon Park. Open Tue–Sun except public hols. Donations.

Built between 1934 and 1938 from five medieval cloisters, chapels, and halls, imported from southern Europe, this spectacular museum of medieval art (a branch of MoMA) houses illuminated manuscripts, tapestries, stained glass, sculptures, enamels, ivories, and paintings, covering Romanesque to Gothic.

Wave Hill ❸

West 249th St and Independence Ave, Riverdale. Open Tue–Sun. Adm charge. Free Tue, Sat am Dec–Feb.

This 28-acre (11-ha) oasis of calm and beauty boasts fine

Interior of the splendid Armor Hall at Wave Hill

views across the Hudson River to the New Jersey Palisades. The house, herb garden, greenhouses, lawns, and woodlands are open to the public. Concerts often take place in the grand Armor Hall (built 1928).

New York Botanical Garden ❹

Kazimiroff Blvd, Bronx River Pkwy (Exit 7W). Open Tue–Sun except public hols. Adm charge. Free Wed, Sat am.

One of the world's largest botanical gardens, this National Historic Landmark of 250 acres (100 ha) includes 48 gardens and plant collections, 50 acres (20 ha) of uncut forest, a glorious Victorian glasshouse, a Children's Adventure Garden, and a conservatory with tropical rain forests and deserts.

Enid A. Haupt Conservatory, New York Botanical Garden

Bronx Zoo/Wildlife Conservation Park ⑤

Fordham Rd, Bronx River Pkwy.
Open daily. Children's Zoo
Apr–Oct. Adm charge. Free Wed.

The US's largest urban zoo (1899) is home to 4,000 animals of 500 species and helps to perpetuate endangered species, such as the Indian rhinoceros and the snow leopard. Its 265 acres (107 ha) of woods, streams, and parklands include a children's zoo and butterfly garden. A shuttle train takes visitors around the sprawling park; the Skyfari cable car gives the best overview.

Brooklyn Children's Museum ⑥

Brooklyn Ave. Open Tue–Fri,
Jul–Aug, Wed–Fri, Sep–Jun except
public hols. Adm charge.

Housed in a hi-tech, specially designed underground building (1976), it is one of the world's most imaginative children's museums. A maze of passageways running off the main "people tube" (a huge drainage pipe connecting four levels), it teaches about other cultures, the planet, and the past.

Brooklyn Academy of Music (BAM) ⑦

Lafayette Ave. Adm charge.

This stately, Neo-Italianate 1908 building, home to the Brooklyn Philharmonic and a leading cultural venue, draws city-wide audiences for its avant-garde program of theater, international music, and dance, especially the Next Wave Festival.

North façade, Brooklyn Museum

Brooklyn Museum ⑧

Eastern Pkwy, Brooklyn. Open
Wed–Sun except public hols.
Donations expected.

This world-class museum, in a fine Beaux Arts building (1897), has some 1.5 million objects, exhibiting cutting-edge contemporary work alongside permanent collections of Egyptian, Asian, American, and African art. There are also Rodin sculptures and decorative arts that include period rooms.

Jamaica Bay Wildlife Refuge Center ⑨

Cross Bay Blvd at Broad Channel.
Open daily sunrise to sunset. Free.

The Refuge's uplands and marshes shelter 300 species of bird, in an area almost the size of Manhattan. On the main Atlantic migratory path, it is at its best in spring and fall, with skies filled with wildfowl. Park rangers lead hikes and nature walks for weekend visitors.

The quiet village of Broad Channel is sheltered by Jamaica Bay

Getting Around

With 6,000 miles (10,000 km) of streets, walking to sites within one area is possible. Yellow cabs get stuck in traffic, as do buses. The subway is quick, reliable, and cheap, but the network can be confusing. Weekly and day passes are valid for all public transportation.

Do not cross the street (left) and You may cross the street (right) signs

Walking

Avenues run north–south, streets east–west. Most intersections have lampposts with name-markers and electric traffic signals. Red is stop for vehicles, green is go, and "Walk–Don't Walk" is for pedestrians. Vehicles keep to the right. Black-and-white markings on many street crossings mean pedestrians have the right of way.

Cycling

Cycling in the city is safest on the park pathways (in Central Park and along the East and Hudson Rivers) during daylight hours.

Ferries

The Circle Line runs several times a day to Ellis Island and the Statue of Liberty from Battery Park at the southern tip of Manhattan. The 24-hour Staten Island ferry from Battery Park travels the channel, giving splendid views of lower Manhattan's skyline and the bridges – and it's free.

Renting a Car

You must be at least 25 years old (or pay a surcharge), with a valid driver's license, a passport (if from overseas), and a credit card. Take out insurance with liability protection and damage cover. Refill the gas before returning the car. Rent in the city, rather than at the airport; it's cheaper. Most bridges charge a toll.

Parking

It's difficult and costly. Use parking garages or your hotel. Some meters allow 20 to 60 minutes; or alternate-side parking on side streets. Never use an out-of-order meter; you'll get a ticket.

Yellow Cabs

Each of the 12,000 licensed Yellow Cabs has a meter, can print a receipt, and will carry up to four people; a single fare covers all. Taxi

New York taxi cab

stands are scarce, so best places are railroad stations or hotels. Cash is preferred and give a 15% tip.

Using the Subway

New York subway logo

The vast system covers 233 route miles (375 km), has 468 stations, and runs 24 hours a day; not all routes operate at all times. The fare is $2 no matter how far you travel. The MetroCard has replaced tokens and is also used on buses. Visitors can buy a one-day FunPass ($7) for unlimited travel all day, a $10 pass (5 rides, 1 free ride), a $20 pass (10 rides, 2 free rides), or a $21 pass (unlimited travel all week). Each station has a subway map (a separate color for each line) and a train timetable for each route. Many entrances are marked by a lit-up sphere (green for 24-hour manned booths, red for restricted entry). Others have a sign giving the name of the station and the numbers or letters of the routes passing through it.

Traveling by Train

Grand Central Terminal has commuter trains to the suburbs and Connecticut. Penn Station has long-distance Amtrak services for the USA and Canada. Path trains operate 24 hours between Penn Station and New Jersey. The Acela express runs between Washington and Boston, via New York. Use cash or credit cards for a one-way fare or a return (twice a single); always buy a ticket before getting on board. Seniors get a 15% discount. Metro-North and LIRR have weekly and off-peak passes. Train times, gate numbers, and destinations are updated on large information boards. Take day trips to Long Island, Connecticut, or Delaware.

Traveling by Bus

Blue-and-white buses cover 200 routes in five boroughs; many run 24 hours a day. You can use a MetroCard or pay by exact coins (not pennies or 50 cents). Disabled and seniors get discounts. Ask the driver for a transfer ticket if taking more than one bus. Bus stops are marked by red, white, and blue signs and yellow paint along the curb. Some serve more than one route; schedules and route maps are posted at each stop. Look for the route number on the lighted strip above the windshield on the front of the bus.

Route numbers appear on the front and side of the bus

Survival Guide

In 1998, New York was rated the safest US city with over a million population. Police concentrate on foot and bicycle patrols in tourist areas. Travel insurance should cover your medical needs. Many international banks have offices here, so changing money is easy.

MONEY

Currency exchange counter

Currency

US currency is dollars and cents (100 cents = 1 dollar). Bills (bank notes) come in $1, $5, $10, $20, $50, and $100; all are green, so be careful. Coins come in 50- (half dollar), 25- (quarter), 10- (dime), 5- (nickel), and 1-cent (penny) pieces, plus a new gold-tone $1 (buck). The new $20 and $50 bills have new larger numbers.

Credit Cards

Mastercard, VISA, American Express, JCB, and Diners Club cards can be used for cash advances. Nearly everything can be paid for by credit card, especially car rentals, hotels, and meals. Using a card avoids having to carry cash.

Cash Dispensers (ATMs)

ATMS (usually Cirrus or Plus networks) are in nearly all bank lobbies, so you can obtain US currency 24 hours a day. Before you travel, check which NYC banks and ATM systems accept your bank card.

Changing Money and Checks

American Express or Thomas Cook traveler's checks in dollars are widely accepted in most shops, hotels, and restaurants. Checks in other currencies must be changed at a bank. It is best to change foreign currency at Travelex Currency Services, Inc. or American Express; expect to pay a fee plus commission. Chase Manhattan Bank has many locations, or use a check-cashing shop.

COMMUNICATIONS

Post Offices

The General Post Office, at 421 8th Avenue, is open 24 hours a day. Letters and postcards can be sent at your hotel, in a post office, or in the red, white, and blue boxes, and all go first class. Buy stamps at post offices or coin-operated machines in pharmacies, stores, and bus and train stations. There are three

Standard mailbox

special mail services: express, priority, overseas.

Telephones

Five area codes are used in New York: 212, 917, 646 for Manhattan, 718 and 347 for other boroughs; 800, 888, and 877 numbers are free. If calling outside your area, first dial 1, then area code, then the number; for inside your area, delete the 1. The standard charge is 25 cents for three minutes in pay phones. The operator will request more money if the call is longer. Prepaid phone cards ($5, $10 or $25) offer substantial savings for long-distance calls.

Sign for public payphones

HEALTH AND SAFETY

Law Enforcement

New York's police department has around-the-clock foot, horse, bike, and car patrols. Call 911 or 0 in an emergency. Police also ride the buses and subway. Guardian Angels (youths in red berets) help patrol midtown streets and subways. Report all crimes or lost property, and keep a copy of the statement that you make to the police.

Travel Insurance

Emergency medical and dental cover is essential, because of high medical costs. Accidental death, dismemberment, baggage and travel document loss and theft, and trip cancellation cover is also important.

Medical Treatment

Health facilities are excellent, but fees are unregulated. A few physicians and dentists accept credit cards; cash or traveler's checks are preferred. Hospitals accept most credit cards.

Pharmacies

Several 24-hour pharmacies operate in the city, such as: Rite Aid, 50th St at 8th Ave. Tel: (212) 247 8384.

MEDICAL EMERGENCIES

In an emergency, telephone an ambulance on 911. Choose a private hospital, rather than a city-owned one; dial **411** for the nearest. Or your hotel can ask a doctor or dentist to make a room call: **NY Hotel Urgent Medical Services** Tel: (212) 737 1212. The Beth Israel Medical Center has three excellent walk-in clinics. One is at: **DOCS**, 55 E 34th St, Tel: (212) 252 6000. Other useful contacts are: **Dial-a-Doctor** Tel: (212) 971 9692. **NYU Dental Care** 345 E 24th St & 1st Ave. Tel: (212) 998 9800 (Mon–Fri); (212) 998 9828 (weekends or after 9pm).
Hospital Emergency Rooms: •St. Vincents, 11th St & 7th Ave. Tel: (212) 604 7998. •St. Luke's Roosevelt, 58th St & 9th Ave. Tel: (212) 523 6800.

A 24-hour pharmacy

Index

Abyssinian Baptist
Church 83
Algonquin Hotel 48
Alice in Wonderland
(statue) 75
American Folk Art
Museum 61
American Museum of
Natural History 6,
75, 81
Andersen, Hans
Christian (statue)
74
Apollo Theater 85
Appellate Division of
the Supreme Court
of the State of New
York 38
Asia Society 70

bars, cafés, and
lounges
Chelsea & Garment
District 45
Lower Midtown 49
Soho & Tribeca 29
Theater District 51
Upper West Side 81
Battery Park 7, 13, 15
Bayard-Condict
Building 35
Belevedere Castle 75,
76
Bethesda Fountain
and Terrace 75, 77
Block Beautiful 39
Bow Bridge 75, 76
Bowling Green 11
Broad Channel 89
Bronx Zoo & Wildlife
Conservation Park
89
Brooklyn Academy
of Music (BAM) 89
Brooklyn Bridge 5,
18
Brooklyn Children's
Museum 89
Brooklyn Museum 89
Bryant Park Hotel 49

cafés see bars, cafés,
and lounges
Canal Street 22
Carnegie Hall 50
Castle Clinton Nat'l
Monument 13
Cathedral of St John
the Divine 84
Central Park 7, 73,
74–75

Central Park Wildlife
Center 74, 77
Central Synagogue
64
Chelsea Hotel 45
Chelsea Piers
Complex 45
Children's Museum
of Manhattan 45
Chinatown 7, 21, 22
Christopher Street 29
Chrysler Building 6,
53, 55
Church of the
Ascension 31
Church of the Holy
Trinity 70
Church of the
Incarnation 56
Citigroup Center 64
City Center of Music
and Dance 50
The Cloisters 88
Colonnade Row 34
Columbia University
84
Con Edison
headquarters 37
Conservatory Garden
77
Conservatory Water
75, 77
Cooper-Hewitt
National Design
Museum 68
Cooper Union 34, 68
Criminal Courts
Building 18

Daily News Building
55
The Dairy 74, 76
Dakota Building 75
Diamond Row 48

East 92nd Street 67
East Seventh Street
33
Eldridge Street
Synagogue 7, 22
Ellis Island 14
Empire Diner 41
Empire State Building
5, 6, 42–43
Engine Company No.
31 (fire station) 23
Enid A. Haupt
Conservatory 88
Federal Hall 10
Federal Reserve Bank
10
Fifth Avenue 60

Flatiron Building 6,
38
Forbes Magazine
Building 30
Fraunces Tavern
Museum 14
Fred F. French
Building 56
Frick Collection 69,
74
Fuller Building 65

General Electric
Building 48
General Post Office
45
George Washington
Bridge 88
Grace Church 35
Gramercy Park 7, 39
Gramercy Park Hotel
39
Grand Central
Terminal 4, 54
Grant's Tomb 84
Greene Street 25, 26
Group Health
Insurance Building
50
Solomon R.
Guggenheim
Museum 6, 69, 75
Gutenberg Bible 57

Hayden Planetarium
81
Home Savings of
America 54

IBM Building 60
International Center
of Photography 49
Intrepid Sea-Air-
Space Museum 51

Jamaica Bay 87, 89
Jamaica Bay Wildlife
Refuge Center 89
Japan Society 56
Jefferson Market
Courthouse 30
Jewish Museum 68
Judson Memorial
Church 31

Let There Be Neon
gallery 27
Liberty Island 13
Lincoln Center for
the Performing Arts
80
Lincoln Center
Theater 80

Acknowledgments

Dorling Kindersley would like to thank the following people whose help and assistance contributed to the preparation of this book.

Design and Editorial

Publisher Douglas Amrine
Publishing Manager Vivien Antwi
Managing Art Editor Kate Poole
Cartography Casper Morris
Design Kavita Saha, Shahid Mahmood
Editorial Dora Whitaker
Production Controller Shane Higgins
Picture Research Ellen Root
DTP Jason Little
Jacket Design Simon Oon, Tessa Bindloss

Picture Credits

Every effort has been made to trace the copyright holders, and we apologize in advance for any omissions. We would be pleased to insert appropriate acknowledgments in any subsequent edition of this publication.

t = top; tl = top left; tc = top centre; tr = top right; cla = centre left above; ca = centre above; cra = centre right above; cl = centre left; c = centre; cr = centre right; clb = centre left below; cb = centre below; crb = centre right below; bl = bottom left; b = bottom; bc = bottom centre; br = bottom right.

The Publishers are grateful to the following individuals, companies and picture libraries for permission to reproduce their photographs:

THE BROOKLYN MUSEUM: Adam Husted 89t; THE TEXT BANK: 5tl; MAGNUM: C. Peres 20; METROPOLITAN TRANSIT AUTHORITY: 91t/b; Collection of THE MORGAN LIBRARY: *Biblia Latina* David A. Loggie 57tl; THE MUSEUM OF MODERN ART, NY: Photography by Elizabeth Felicella, architectural rendering by Kohn Penderson Fox Associates, digital composite by Robert Bowen Digital Image 58; ©Timothy Hursely 61cl.

JACKET
Front – GETTY IMAGES: Stone/Joseph Pobereskin
Spine – DK IMAGES: Dave King

All other images © DORLING KINDERSLEY
For further information see www.DKimages.com.

Price Codes are for a three-course meal per person including tax, a 15–20% tip, and half a bottle of house wine
Cheap under $25
Moderate $25–$50
Expensive $50 or more

SPECIAL EDITIONS OF DK TRAVEL GUIDES

DK Travel Guides can be purchased in bulk quantities at discounted prices for use in promotions or as premiums. We are also able to offer special editions and personalized jackets, corporate imprints, and excerpts from all of our books, tailored specifically to meet your own needs. To

fTo find out more, please contact:
(in the United States)
SpecialSales@dk.com
(in the UK) **Sarah.Burgess@dk.com**
(in Canada) DK Special Sales at
general@tourmaline.ca
(in Australia) **business.development@pearson.com.au**

Little Italy 7, 22
lounges see bars, cafés, and lounges
Low Library 84
Lower East Side Tenement Museum 22
Lyceum Theater 48

McSorley's Old Ale House 33
Macy's 44
Madison Square 7, 38
Madison Square Garden 44
Manhattan 4–5
Marble Collegiate Reformed Church 44
Merchant's House Museum 34
MetLife Building 54
Metropolitan Life Insurance Company 38
Metropolitan Museum of Art 6, 69, 75
Metropolitan Opera House 80
Morgan Library 5, 57
Mount Vernon Hotel Museum 70
Municipal Building 18, 19
Museo del Barrio 85
Museum of Arts & Design 61
Museum of the City of New York 71
Museum of Jewish Heritage 15
Museum of Modern Art 6, 59, 61
Museum of Television and Radio 61

National Academy Museum 68
Neue Galerie New York 68
New Amsterdam Theater 50
New Museum of Contemporary Art 26
New York Botanical Garden 88
New York City Fire Museum 26
New York Earth Room 26

New-York Historical Society 81
New York Public Library 49
New York State Theater 80
New York Stock Exchange 10

Patchin Place 30
Police Headquarters Building 22
Public Theater 34
Puck Building 23

restaurants
    Chelsea & Garment District 45
    East Village 35
    Empire Diner 41
    Four Seasons 64, 65
    Gramercy & Flatiron District 39
    Greenwich Village 31
    Lower East Side 23
    Lower Manhattan 15
    Lower Midtown 57
    Morningside Heights & Harlem 85
    Seaport & Civic Center 19
    Soho & Tribeca 27
    Sylvia's 7, 85
    Theater District 51
    Upper East Side 71
    Upper Midtown 65
    Upper West Side 81
Riverside Church 84
Riverside Drive 79
Rockefeller Center 48
Theodore Roosevelt Birthplace 39
Roosevelt Island 65

St. Elizabeth Ann Seton Shrine 11
St. John the Baptist Church 44
St. Luke's Place 30
St. Mark's-in-the-Bowery Church 35
St. Nicholas Russian Orthodox Cathedral 7, 71
St. Patrick's Cathedral 62–63
St. Paul's Chapel 19
St. Thomas Church 60

San Remo 75, 80
Schermerhorn Row 18
Seagram Building 64
Seventh Avenue South 29
Seventh Regiment Armory 70
Sheridan Square 7, 30
shopping
    Fifth Avenue 57, 60
    Lower East Side 23
    Lower Midtown 57
    Macy's 44
    Upper East Side 71
    Upper Midtown 65
Shubert Alley 50
Shubert Theater 50
Singer Building 26
Society of Illustrators 70
South Street Seaport 17, 18
Staten Island Ferry 14
Statue of Liberty 4, 6, 12–13
Strawberry Fields 74, 76
Studio Museum in Harlem 85
Surrogate's Court, Hall of Records 19
Sylvia's 7, 85

Times Square 47, 49
Trinity Church 9, 10
Trump Tower 7, 60
Tudor City 55
Twin Towers of Central Park West 80

United Nations 56
US Custom House 11

Vietnam Veterans' Plaza 14
Villard Houses 64

Waldorf-Astoria 64
Wave Hill 88
White Street 27
Whitney Museum of American Art 6, 69
Winter Garden 11
Wollman Rink 74
Woolworth Building 19
World Financial Center 11
Worth Monument 45